Making Toys

Heirloom Cars & Trucks in Wood

REVISED EDITION

Sam Martin & Roger Schroeder

Measured Drawings by John Nelson

FOX CHAPEL
PUBLISHING

DEDICATION

Dedicated to our wives, Georgia Martin and Sheila Schroeder,

for their love and support; and to our publisher,

who made this project possible

The following images are credited to Shutterstock.com and their respective creators: wood texture throughout, monofaction; wood texture bottom of pages 4–5, kamon_saejueng.

ISBN 978-1-4971-0116-6

Library of Congress Control Number: 2020936321

To learn more about the other great books from Fox Chapel Publishing, or to find a retailer near you, call toll-free 800-457-9112 or visit us at *www.FoxChapelPublishing.com*.

We are always looking for talented authors. To submit an idea, please send a brief inquiry to acquisitions@foxchapelpublishing.com.

Printed in China
Second printing

INTRODUCTION

Sam Martin's reproductions of trucks, vintage cars, locomotives, and earth movers captured my interest as soon as I lay eyes on their scaled details and smooth surfaces of contrasting woods. I was impressed with the craftsmanship because, like Sam, I am a woodworker. It was soon after I met Sam that the collaboration for this book began in his workshop in Lancaster, Pennsylvania.

Sam's shop consists of a variety of tools for making toys. His cutting tools are a table saw, band saw, and radial arm saw. A jointer is available for truing an edge. He has a lathe for turning wood and a thickness planer for reducing the thickness of a board. He uses a router table for putting curved profiles on wood and dadoes and rabbets into the lumber. His sanding equipment consists of stationary belt and disc sanders and an oscillating drum sander. And his hand tools are varied enough to move a project along quickly.

All of these tools will make your job of reproducing Sam's designs a pleasure, although you will be able to do without some and you may well have others that are more efficient.

Sam does not choose fancy joinery to lock the components of his toys together. Most of the pieces are butted and glued. Time has taught Sam that his carpenter's glue is strong and stable and keeps the toys together even when they are played with vigorously. Nails are used only to secure lights, stacks, airhorns, and other cylinders to his cars and trucks.

I was surprised, however, to find that Sam employs no plans or blueprints. Working from photographs, he experiments with proportions until he arrives at a scale with which he is comfortable. When he wants to fabricate more of the same toy, he takes measurements off one previously made.

The toys—which Sam began calling collectibles—described on the following pages were all crafted in oak and walnut. Other woods—cherry, maple, mahogany—can easily be substituted. In fact, Sam often uses cherry to fashion some of his vehicles.

It is our intent to present pictorially the making of a truck and trailer, allowing you to see how to make the parts and put them together. The primary wood is oak; the contrasting wood is walnut. The rest of the book is devoted to plans for a flatbed trailer that can be substituted for the enclosed trailer; a 1932 Buick with running boards, a spare tire, and passenger seats; and a Ford pickup dating to the 1930s.

It was a great pleasure working with Sam for a week in the August of 1996. I was impressed with his speed, his economy of movements, and, of course, the beautiful truck and trailer he produced. I hope you will be as inspired as I was to buy the wood necessary, turn on the power tools, and make toys that, I suspect, will last at least a lifetime and hopefully more.

Roger Schroeder
Amityville, New York

CONTENTS

PROJECT GALLERY

Projects in the Book

This is the featured step-by-step project, the Peterbilt Truck. Patterns start on page 14, and you can follow along with the complete building process in 155 steps starting on page 34.

The Flatbed Trailer fits behind the Peterbilt Truck tractor. (Patterns and details starting on page 103.)

The Ford Model A Pickup—a classic for more than half a century—is an ideal project for the woodworker beginning to build Sam's wooden replicas. (Patterns and details starting on page 90.)

1932 Buick Sedan. (Patterns and details starting on page 77.)

Project Inspiration

This backhoe uses a series of springs to give an impressively realistic hydraulic system effect.

This pumper truck is impressive in either of Sam Martin's favorite woods—oak or cherry.

A hallmark of Sam's toys is that every individual piece is made from wood, even down to the Mack emblem made of wooden veneer.

Measuring over 3 feet long, this rig of truck tractor, flatbed trailer, and track backhoe is an impressive sight on the mantle. Using a unique rawhide system, the tracks actually work.

The boom and bucket move and pivot, the cab rotates, and the tracks function.

This cattle truck features a tambour roll-up door just like its real counterpart.

Rear view of the cattle truck.

PETERBILT TRUCK

Learn how to build this rig through the series of step-by-step techniques in this chapter. A complete set of measured drawings follow before the instructions kick off.

The small details are what speak of quality throughout your heirloom toy project.

Notice the working roll-up tambour door and the finishing touches on the back of the van trailer.

Front end angle.

Notice the detail elements and accessories—all made from contrasting hardwoods.

Front view.

Side view.

Truck Parts List

PIECE #	PIECE	SIZE (INCHES)	QUANTITY
1	Base	¾ × 3¼ × 14 ¹¹⁄₁₆	1
2	Rear Axle Housing	⁹⁄₁₆ × 1½ × 9	1
3	Support	¹¹⁄₁₆ × ¹¹⁄₁₆ × 3¼	1
4	Rear Bumper	⁵⁄₁₆ × ¹¹⁄₁₆ × 5¼	1
5	Mud Flap	¹⁄₁₆ × 1¾ × 1⅞	2
6	Axle Holder	¹¹⁄₁₆ × ¾ × 3¾	1
7	Bumper	⁵⁄₁₆ × ¾ × 5¾	1
8	Hood	2 × 3¼ × 3¼	1
9	Firewall	¾ × 2 × 4	1
10	Dash	¾ × 1¼ × 3	1
11	Cab Side	⅜ × 3⁵⁄₁₆ × 3⅝	2
12	Grab Bars	⅛ × ⁵⁄₁₆ × 2	2
13	Back Wall	⅜ × 3¼ × 3⁵⁄₁₆	1
14	Windshield Bar	⅛ Dia. × 1⅞	1
15	Seat Back	⅜ × 2¼ × 3¼	1
16	Seat	¾ × ¹⁵⁄₁₆ × 3¼	1
17	Roof	⁷⁄₁₆ × 4 × 4	1
18	Shade	⁷⁄₁₆ × ¹⁵⁄₁₆ × 4	1
19	Base	⅛ × 1 × 3½	1
20	Stack	⅝ Dia. × 5⅛	2
21	Hitch Wheel	2 Dia. × ⁷⁄₁₆	1
22	Spacer	⅛ × 1⁵⁄₁₆ × 4½	2
23	Fender	1 × 2¹⁄₁₆ × 3⅛	2
24	Grill Top	³⁄₁₆ × ⁷⁄₁₆ × 3¼	1
25	Grill Bottom	³⁄₁₆ × ⅛ × 3¼	1
26	Grill Side	³⁄₁₆ × ³⁄₁₆ × 2³⁄₁₆	2
27	Grill Dividers	³⁄₁₆ × ⅛ × 2³⁄₁₆	3
28	Radiator	³⁄₁₆ × 2¼ × 2³⁄₁₆	1
29	Step Top	¾ × ¹⁵⁄₁₆ × 2½	2
30	Step Bottom	⅛ × 1⅜ × 2½	2
31	Air Tank	½ Dia. × 2½	2
32	Gas Tank	1⁵⁄₁₆ Dia. × 2¼	2
33	Air Cleaner	⅞ Dia. × 1⁹⁄₁₆	2
34	Light Support	¼ × ½ × 1⅛	2
35	Light	⅜ Dia. × ¹⁄₁₆	4
36	Paneling Nail	¹⁄₁₆ Dia. × ¾	2
37	Axle (Short)	⅜ Dia. × 5¾	2
38	Axle (Long)	⅜ Dia. × 2⅝	4
39	Wheel Front	2¼ Dia. × ¹⁵⁄₁₆	2
40	Wheel Back	2¼ Dia. × ¹⁵⁄₁₆	8
41	Lamp	¼ Dia. × ⁵⁄₁₆	5
42	Air Horn	½ Dia. × 1 ¹³⁄₁₆	2
43	Steering Wheel	1⁹⁄₁₆ × ⅞	1
44	Column	¼ Dia. × 1¼	1
45	Axle Cap	⅜ Dia. Dowel Button	6
46	Paneling Nails		As Required

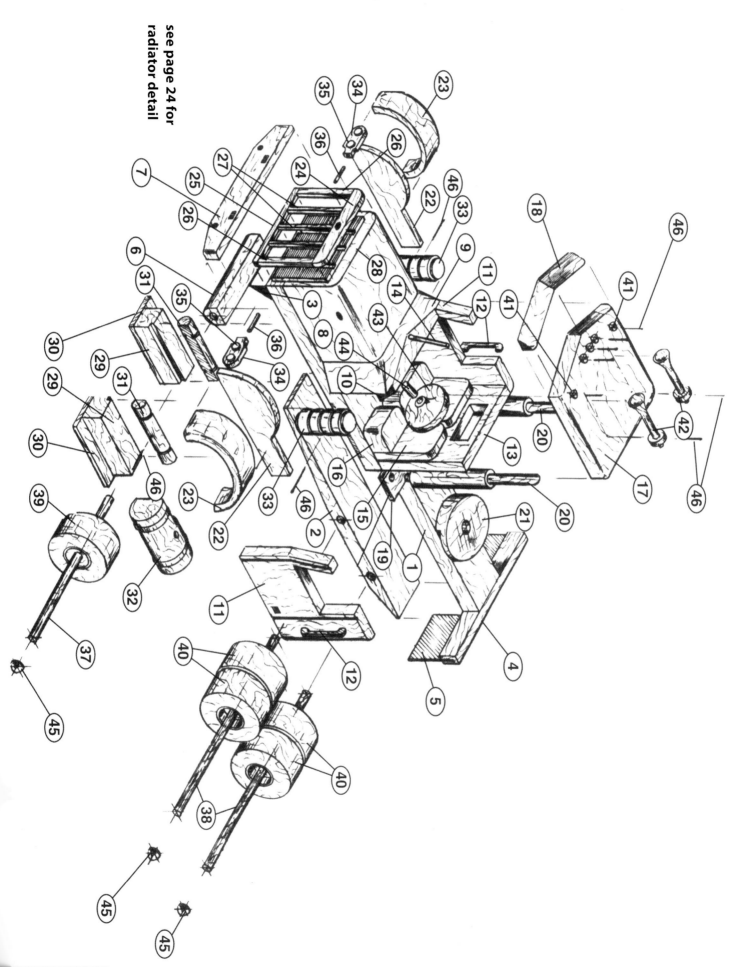

see page 24 for
radiator detail

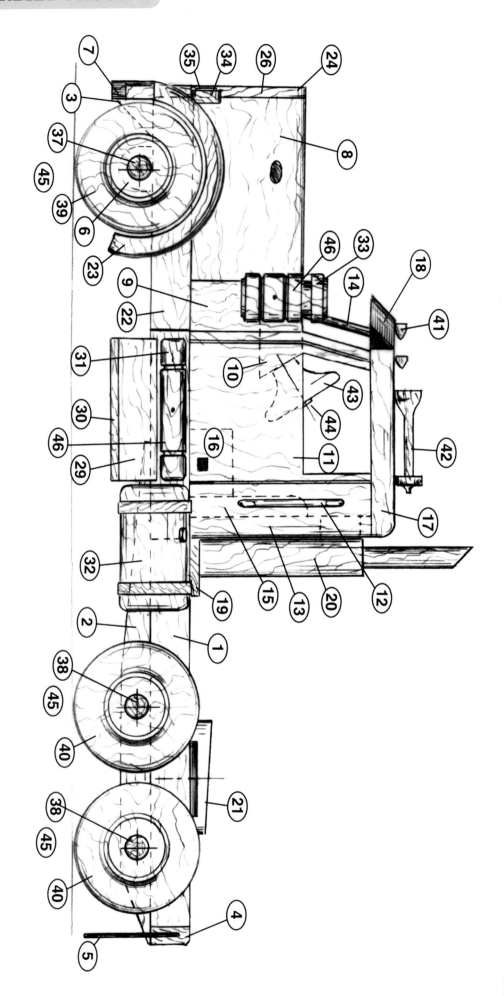

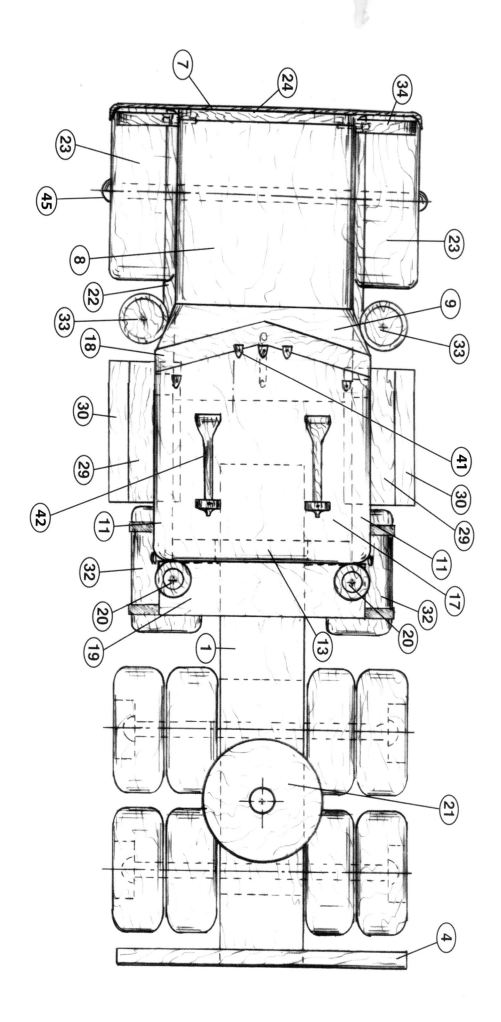

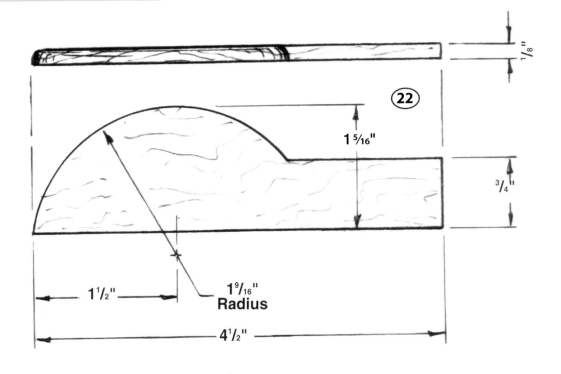

1/8"

(22)

1 5/16"

3/4"

1 1/2"

1 9/16"
Radius

4 1/2"

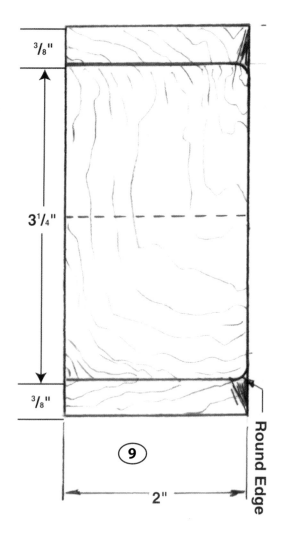

3/8"

3 1/4"

3/8"

(9)

2"

Round Edge

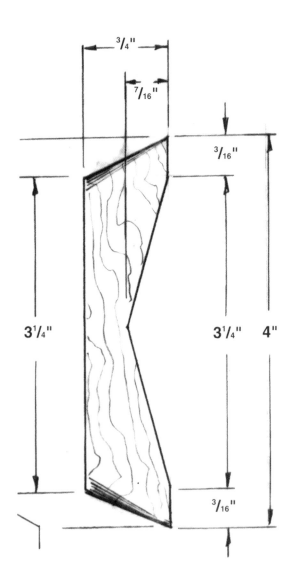

3/4"

7/16"

3/16"

3 1/4"

3 1/4" 4"

3/16"

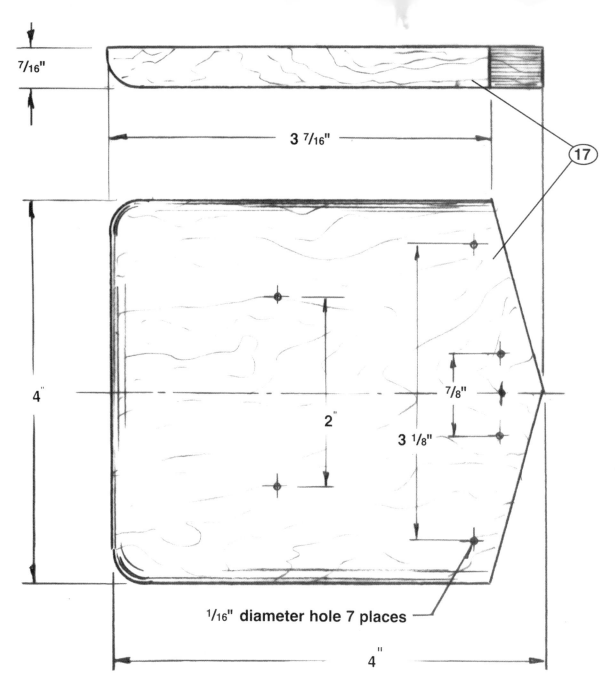

7/16"

3 7/16"

17

4"

2"

7/8"

3 1/8"

1/16" diameter hole 7 places

4"

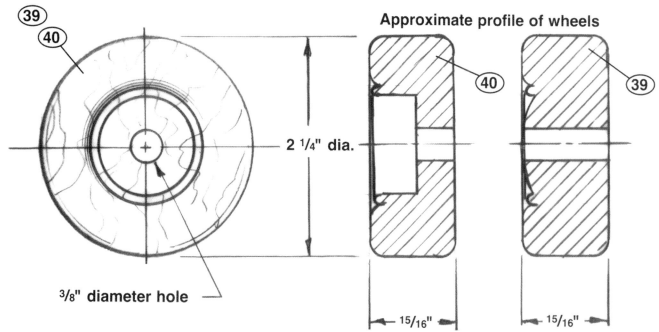

39
40

Approximate profile of wheels

40

39

2 1/4" dia.

3/8" diameter hole

15/16"

15/16"

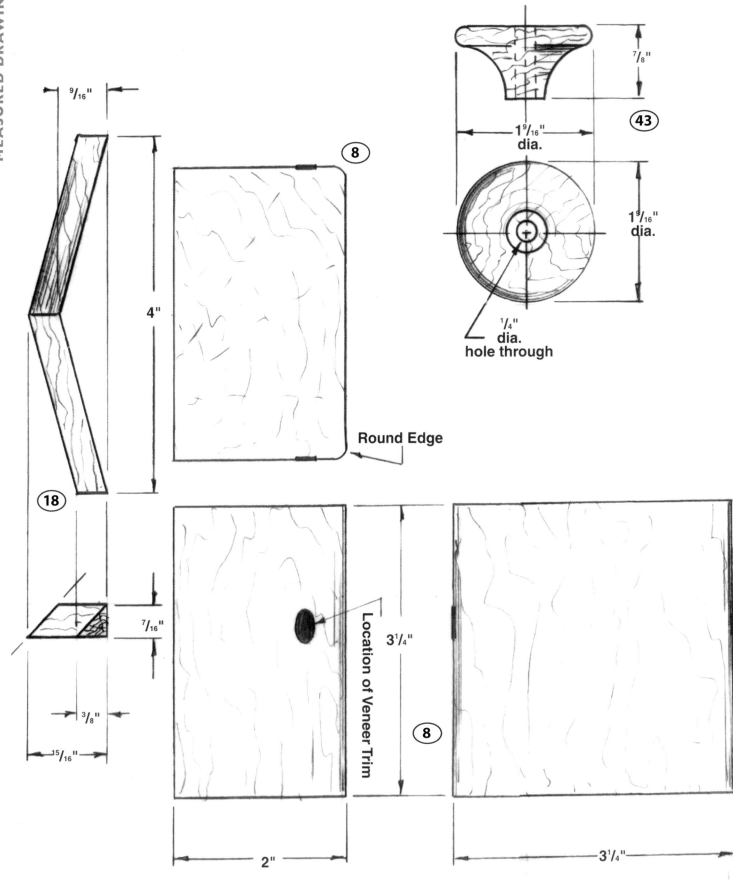

9/16"

4"

18

7/16"

3/8"

15/16"

8

Round Edge

Location of Veneer Trim

3 1/4"

2"

3 1/4"

7/8"

43

1 9/16"
dia.

1 9/16"
dia.

1/4"
dia.
hole through

8

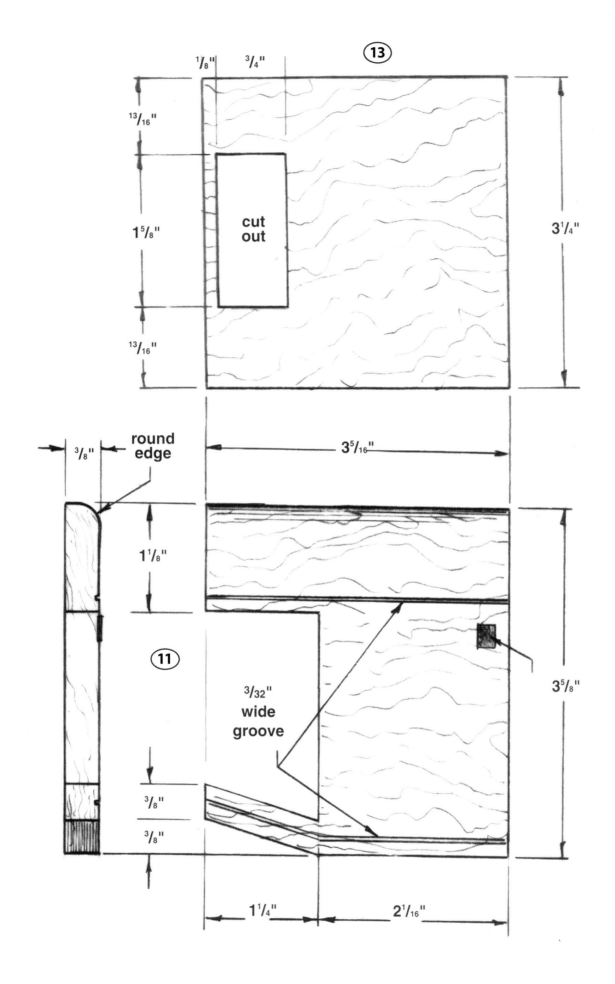

⑬

¹/₈"   ³/₄"

¹³/₁₆"

1 ⁵/₈"

cut out

¹³/₁₆"

3¹/₄"

³/₈"

round edge

3⁵/₁₆"

1¹/₈"

⑪

³/₃₂" wide groove

³/₈"

³/₈"

3⁵/₈"

1¹/₄"

2¹/₁₆"

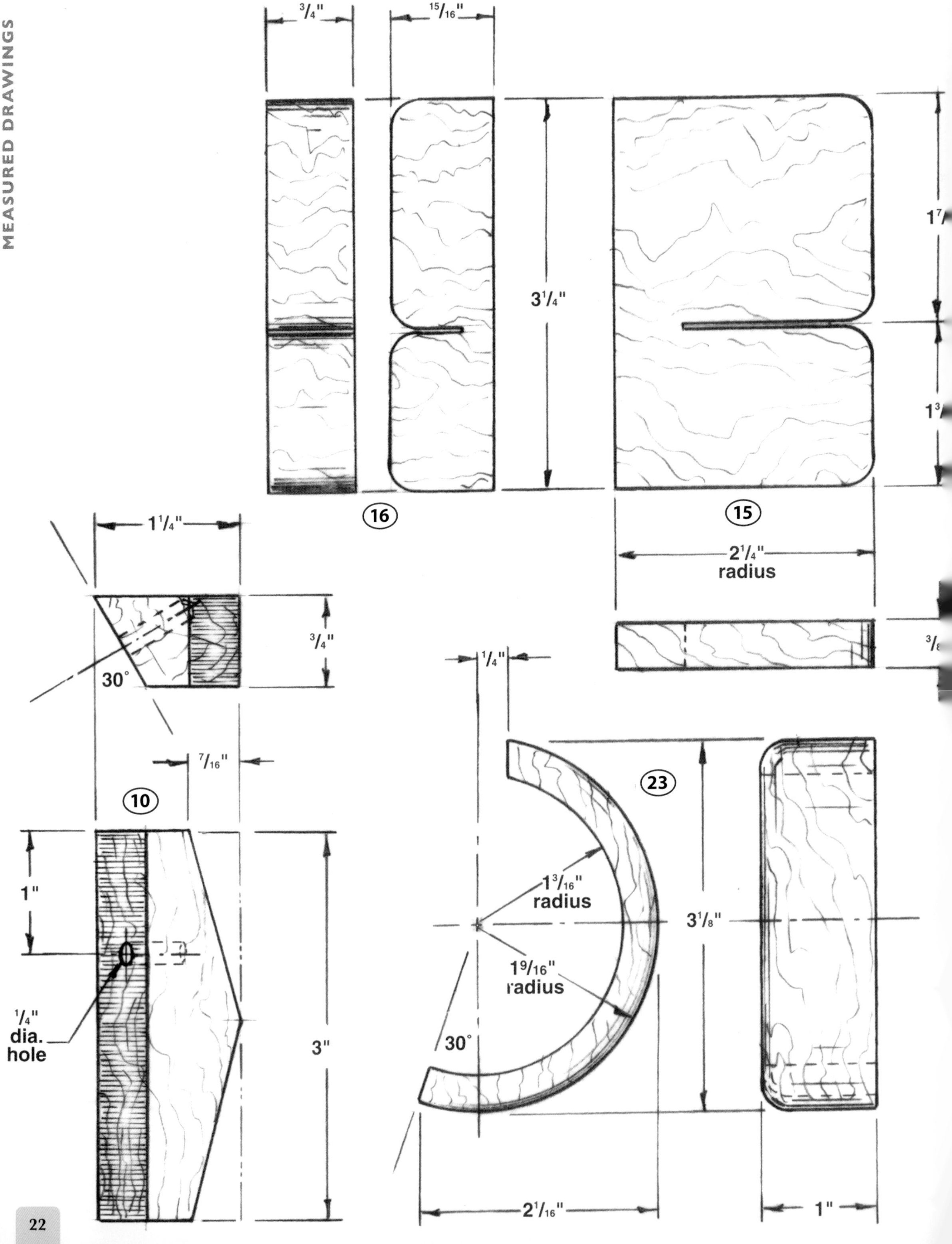

3/4"

15/16"

3 1/4"

1 7/

1 3/

(16)

(15)

2 1/4"
radius

1 1/4"

3/4"

30°

7/16"

3/8

(10)

1"

1/4"
dia.
hole

3"

1/4"

(23)

1 3/16"
radius

1 9/16"
radius

30°

3 1/8"

2 1/16"

1"

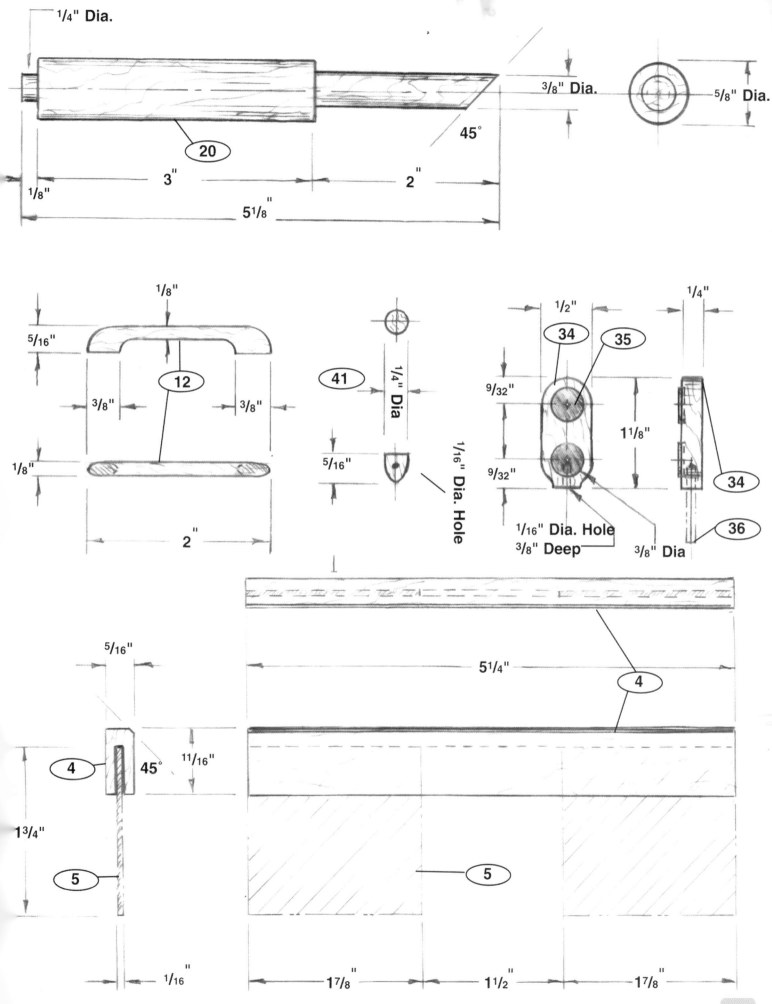

¹/₄" Dia.

³/₈" Dia.

⁵/₈" Dia.

45°

20

3"

2"

5¹/₈"

¹/₈"

¹/₈"

⁵/₁₆"

³/₈"

³/₈"

¹/₈"

12

2"

41

¹/₄" Dia

⁵/₁₆"

¹/₁₆" Dia. Hole

¹/₂"

34

35

9/32"

1¹/₈"

9/32"

¹/₄"

34

36

¹/₁₆" Dia. Hole
³/₈" Deep

³/₈" Dia

⁵/₁₆"

4

5¹/₄"

4

4

45°

11/16"

1³/₄"

5

5

¹/₁₆"

1⁷/₈"

1¹/₂"

1⁷/₈"

PETERBILT TRUCK

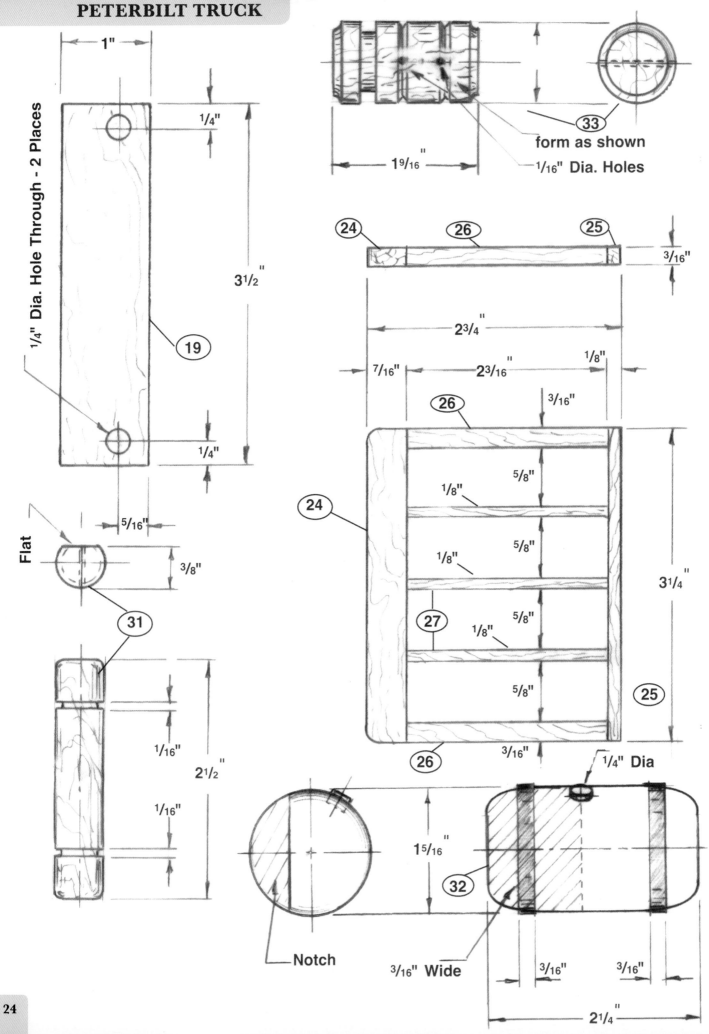

1"

1/4"

3¹/₂"

1/4" Dia. Hole Through - 2 Places

19

1/4"

⁵/₁₆"

Flat

3/8"

31

1/16"

2¹/₂"

1/16"

1⁹/₁₆"

form as shown

1/16" Dia. Holes

33

24   26   25

3/16"

2³/₄"

7/16"   2³/₁₆"   1/8"

26   3/16"

5/8"

1/8"

5/8"

1/8"

5/8"

27

1/8"

24

3¹/₄"

25

5/8"

26   3/16"

Notch

³/₁₆" Wide

1⁵/₁₆"

32

1/4" Dia

3/16"   3/16"

2¹/₄"

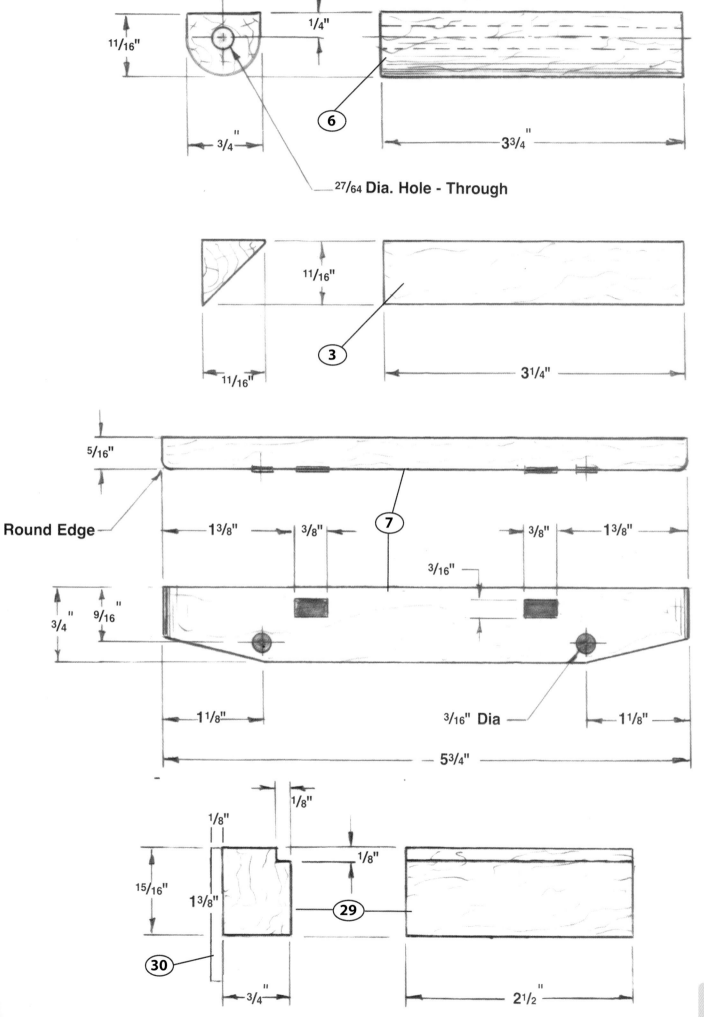

11/16"

1/4"

3/4"

3³/₄"

⑥

²⁷/₆₄ Dia. Hole - Through

11/16"

③

11/16"

3¹/₄"

5/16"

Round Edge

1³/₈"   3/8"   ⑦   3/8"   1³/₈"

3/16"

3/4"   9/16"

3/16" Dia

1¹/₈"   1¹/₈"

5³/₄"

1/8"

1/8"

1/8"

15/16"

1³/₈"

㉙

㉚

3/4"   2¹/₂"

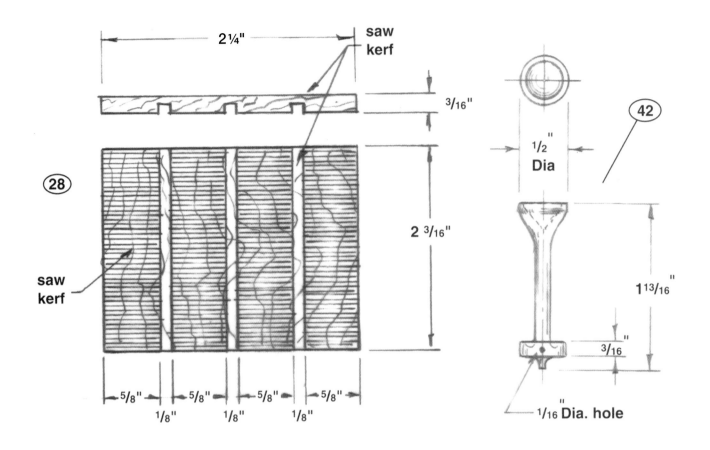

28

saw kerf

saw kerf

2¼"

3/16"

2 3/16"

5/8"   5/8"   5/8"   5/8"

1/8"   1/8"   1/8"

42

½" Dia

1¹³/₁₆"

3/16"

1/16" Dia. hole

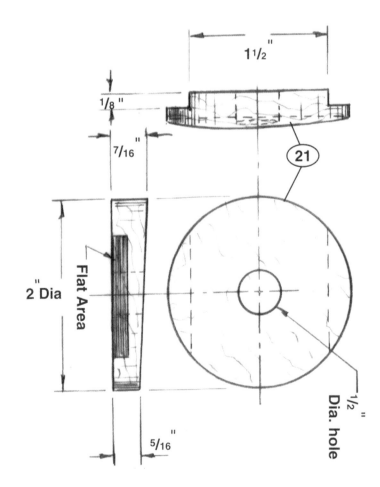

21

1½"

1/8"

7/16"

2" Dia

Flat Area

5/16"

½" Dia. hole

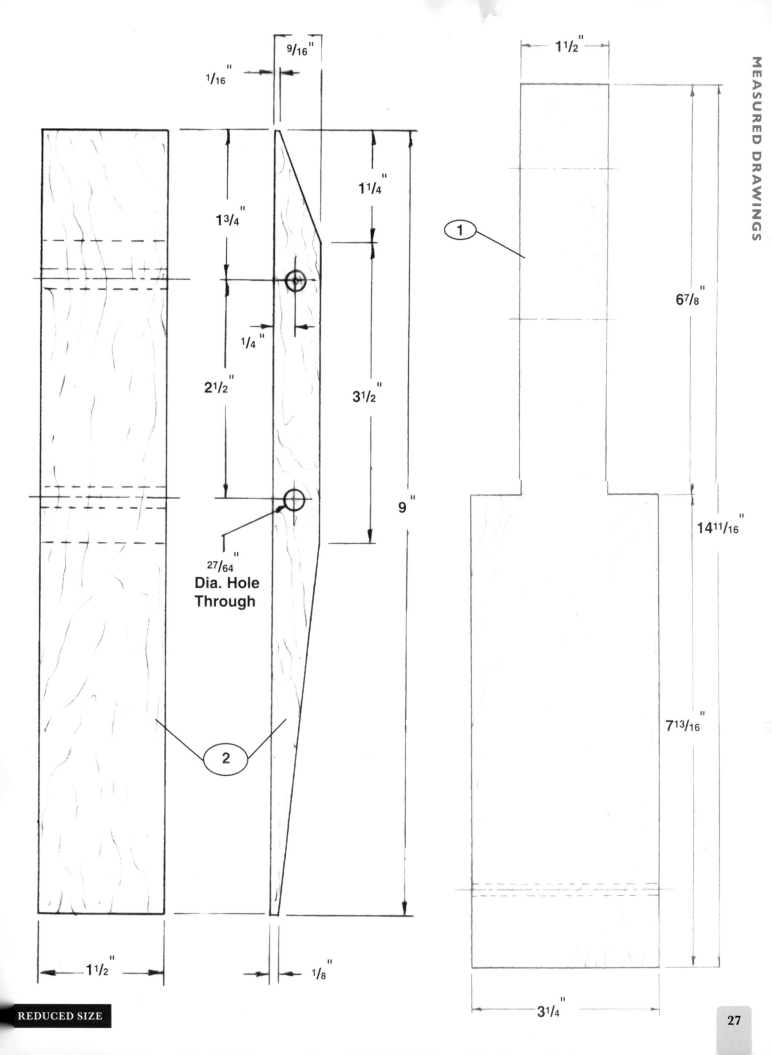

Van Trailer Parts List

PIECE #	PIECE	SIZE (INCHES)	QUANTITY
1	Base	½ × 6 × 22⅞	1
2	Front	1 × 6 × 6⅛	1
3	Side	½ × 5⅝ × 22⅞	2
4	Top	½ × 6 × 23⅞	1
5	Bumper	⁷/₁₆ × ¹¹/₁₆ × 6	1
6	Axle Housing	1¾ × 1⅞ × 11	1
7	Tail Light	⁵/₁₆ Dia. × ¹/₁₆	4
8	Extension	⁵/₁₆ × ⁷/₁₆ × 1¼	2
9	Stop	⅛ × ½ × 2⅜	1
10	Holder	⅜ × ½ × 2	2
11	Mud Flap	¹/₃₂ × 2 × 2 (rubber)	2
12	Trailer Hitch	⁷/₁₆ × 1⅜	1
13	Leg	⅜ × ⁵/₁₆ × 1¾	2
14	Bar	⅛ Dia. × 3¾	1
15	Top Brace	⅛ × ⁹/₁₆ × 1¼	2
16	Bottom Brace	⅛ × ⁵/₁₆ × ¹¹/₁₆	4
17	Foot	⅛ × ¾ × ¾	2
18	Side Frame	³/₁₆ × ½ × 5⅜	2
19	Top Frame	³/₁₆ × ¾ × 6	1
20	Door (End)	¼ × ⅝ × 5¼	2
21	Door Center	¼ × ⅜ × 5¼	13
22	Wheel	2¼ Dia. × ¹⁵/₁₆	10
23	Axle (Short)	⅜ Dia. × 1¼	2
24	Axle (Long)	⅜ Dia. × 3¼	4
25	Door Handle	¹/₁₆ × ⅛ × ⅜	1
26	Door Liner	¹/₃₂ × 4⅞ × 6	1
27	Cap	⅜ Dia. Dowel Button	6
2a*	Front Support	½ x 5¼ x 5½	1
21a*	Door Spacers	⅛ x ¼ x 5⅜	2

*Parts not shown in drawings.

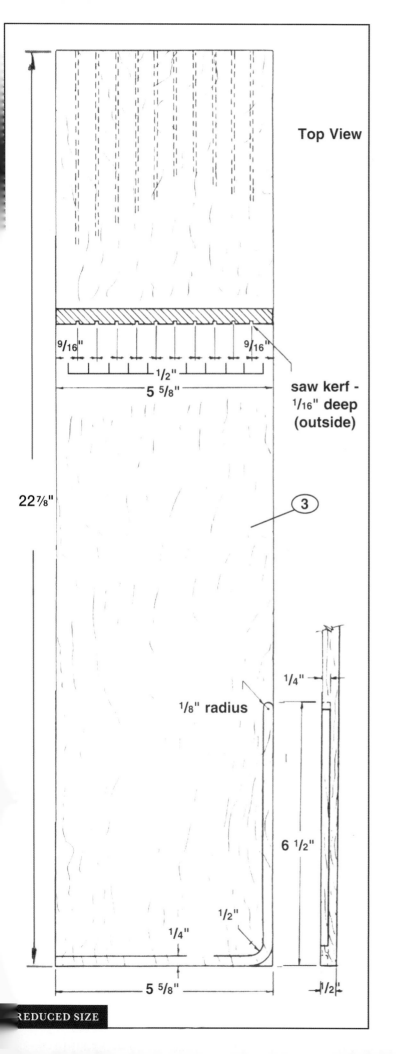

Top View

9/16" 9/16"

1/2"

5 5/8"

saw kerf -
1/16" deep
(outside)

22 7/8"

3

1/8" radius

1/4"

6 1/2"

1/2"

1/4"

5 5/8"

1/2"

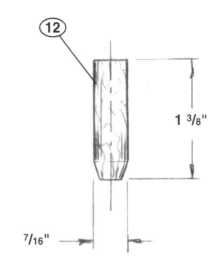

12

1 3/8"

7/16"

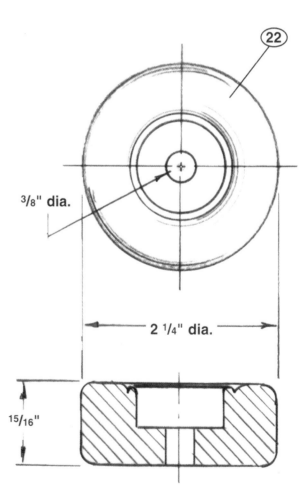

22

3/8" dia.

2 1/4" dia.

15/16"

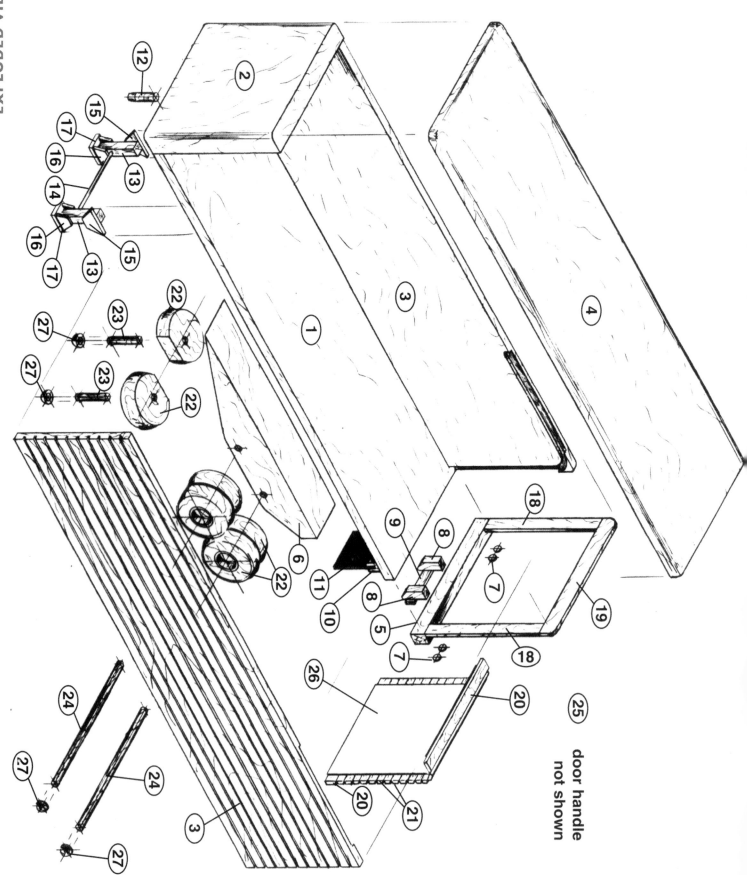

door handle
not shown

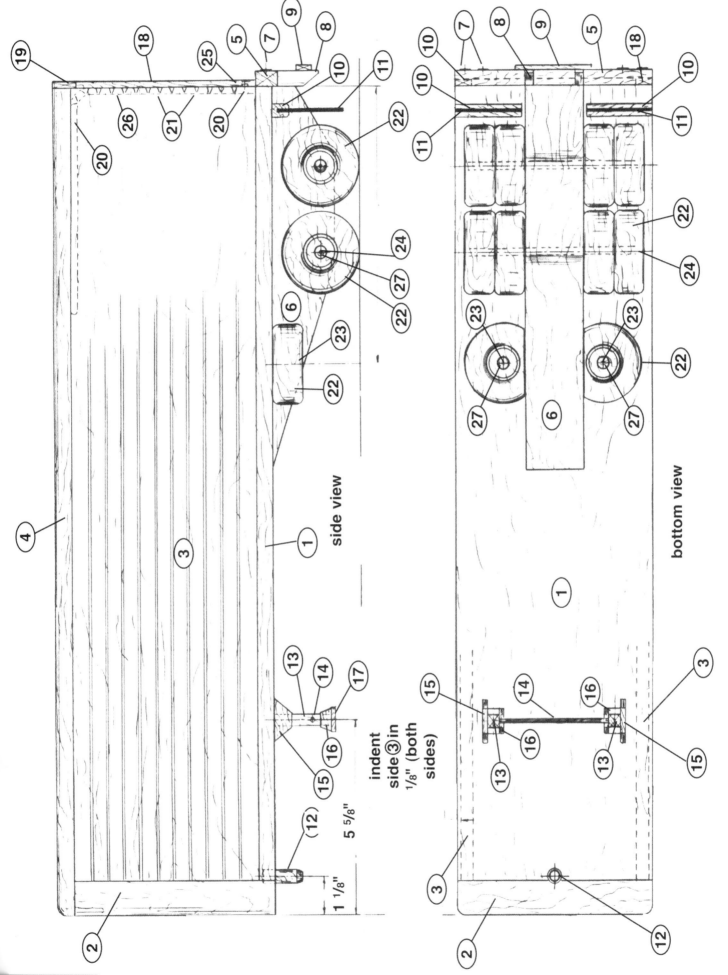

side view

bottom view

indent side ③ in ¹/₈" (both sides)

5 ⁵/₈"

1 ¹/₈"

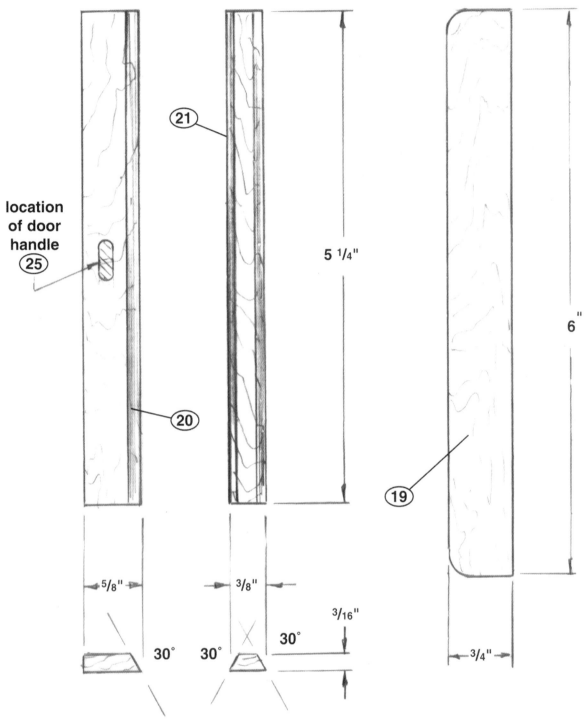

location of door handle ㉕

㉑

㉚

5 1/4"

6"

5/8"

3/8"

30°

30°

30°

3/16"

㉙

3/4"

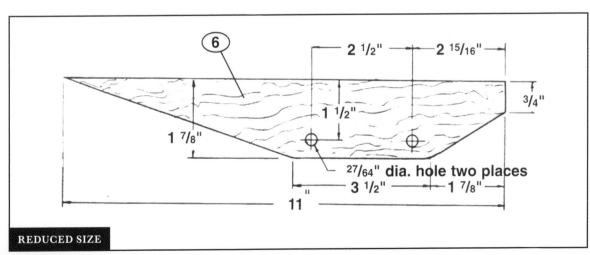

⑥

2 1/2"

2 15/16"

3/4"

1 1/2"

1 7/8"

27/64" dia. hole two places

3 1/2"

1 7/8"

11"

REDUCED SIZE

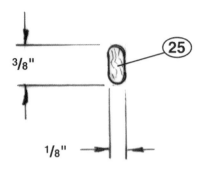

3/8"

1/8"

25

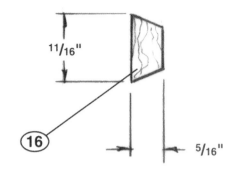

11/16"

16

5/16"

**saw kerf,
3/8" deep**

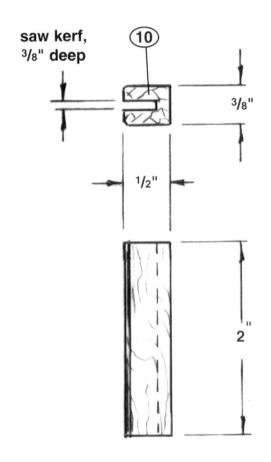

10

3/8"

1/2"

2"

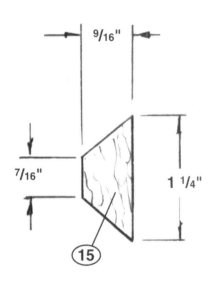

9/16"

7/16"

1 1/4"

15

13

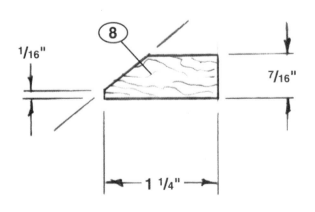

8

1/16"

7/16"

1 1/4"

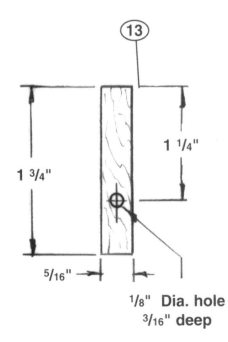

1 3/4"

1 1/4"

5/16"

**1/8" Dia. hole
3/16" deep**

PETERBILT TRUCK

Cut the hood (8) and base (1) to size. Glue them together.

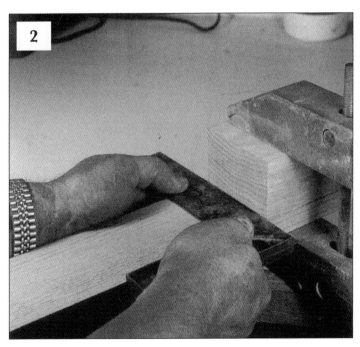

Use a try square to make sure the hood edge is perpendicular to the base.

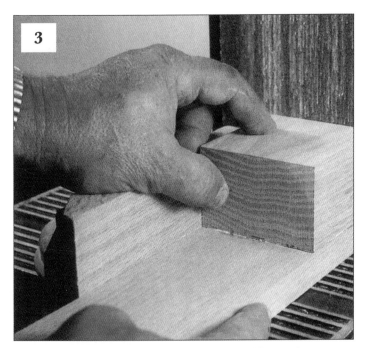

True up the edges of the assembled hood and base using a benchtop belt sander.

The large belt sander smooths the edges of long boards.

Begin work on the radiator (28), which is on the front of the hood. Using a contrasting wood such as walnut, cut ⅛"-wide grooves halfway through ⅜" stock. These grooves will be filled with strips identical to the wood used for the body of the truck.

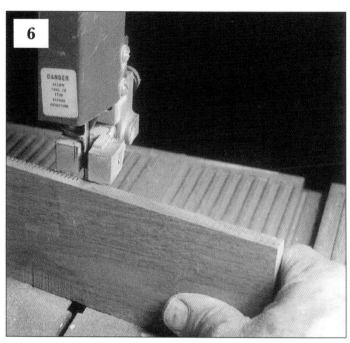

The radiator has horizontal grooves. Use a band saw to make kerf cuts ⅛" apart. Saw no more than halfway into the wood.

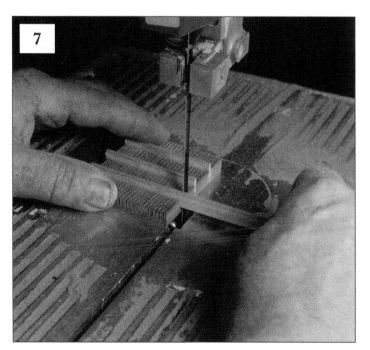

After fitting the dividers (27) into the ⅛"-wide grooves in the radiator, trim off the excess.

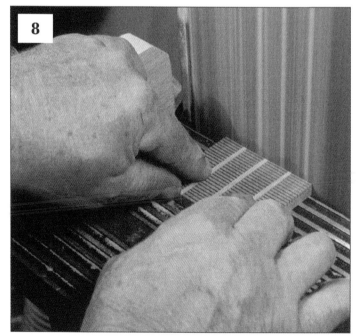

Use the belt sander to make the edges flush.

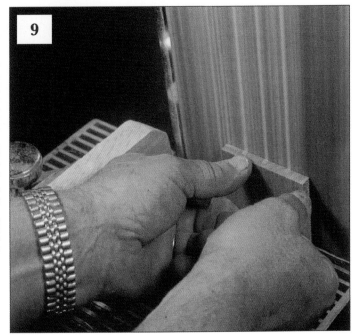

Use the belt sander to smooth the face of the grill.

Attach the grill sides (26) to the radiator. Cut the pieces oversized for easier gluing. Then, cut and sand them to the correct length and width later. Since you are gluing side grain to end grain, consider using epoxy or reinforcing the joint with brads or small dowels.

Glue and clamp the top (24) and bottom (25) to the radiator. Since you want the grain to run vertically on these pieces, you are gluing end grain to side grain. For the strongest joint, use epoxy, or reinforce the joint with brads or small dowels.

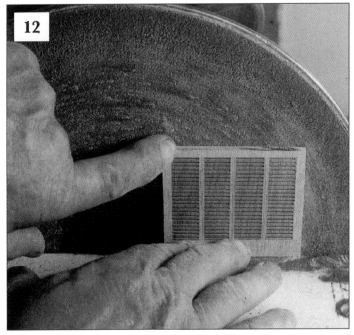

Use a disc sander to make the edges of the grill assembly smooth and flush.

Fit the grill assembly to the front of the hood and glue it in place. Since you are gluing side grain to end grain, reinforce or use epoxy. After the glue has set, sand the edges flush.

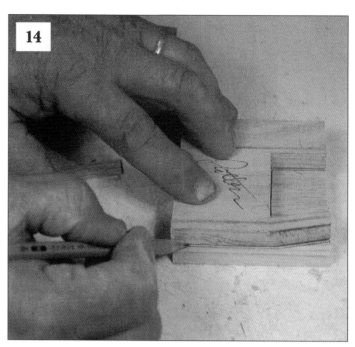

Transfer the pattern to the cab sides (11). Make sure the grain runs vertically.

Use the band saw to cut out the windows. A scroll saw will also do the job.

Remove the band saw marks with a 1" belt sander.

PETERBILT TRUCK

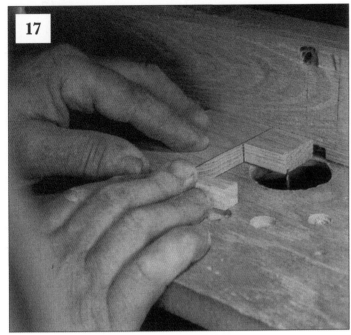

Cut a ³⁄₃₂"-wide groove to indicate the outline of the doors. Use a router table with a ³⁄₃₂" veiner bit.

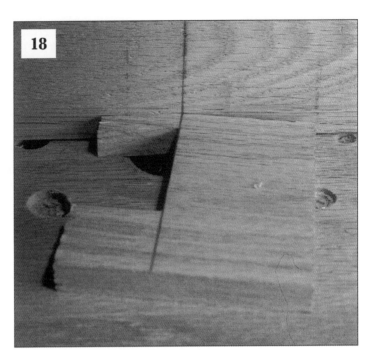

Because one edge of the door front does not have a straight profile, the groove will have to follow the angled edge. Make a mark on the router table fence where the two angles of the door come together. Make another mark on the side in line with the base of the window. When the two marks line up, rotate the side so that it is flat against the fence; push it until the router bit exits at the bottom of the cab side.

Cut the cab back (13) to size. Set your saw at 2 degrees to make the outer edges slant inward. This causes the sides to taper in slightly. Return the saw to square, and cut along the line at the top of the window. Then, cut the open window.

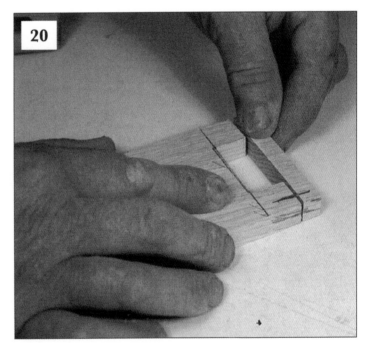

Reattach the piece on the top of the window frame. Make sure the grain is oriented vertically. Since you'll be gluing end grain to end grain, use epoxy or reinforce the joint with brads or small dowels.

Glue the cab sides to the back.

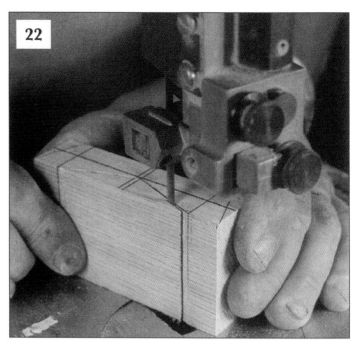

Cut the firewall (9) to shape. Use the band saw.

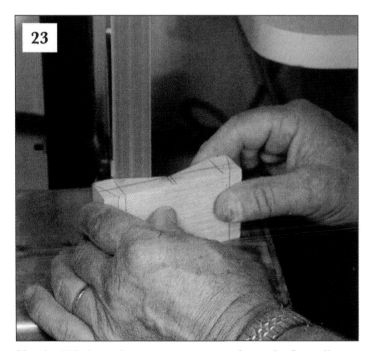

Use the 1" belt sander to remove saw marks on the firewall.

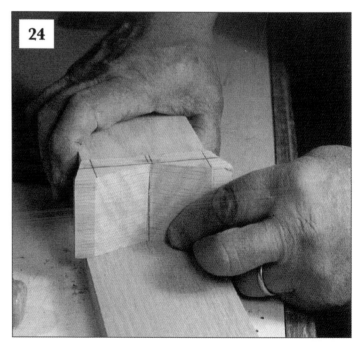

Fit the firewall to the rear of the hood.

25

Use a ¼" roundover bit on the top of the hood and radiator grill assembly.

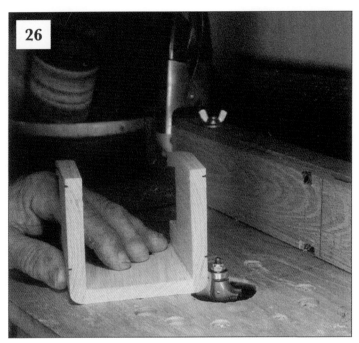

26

Round over the rear edges of the cab with the ¼" bit.

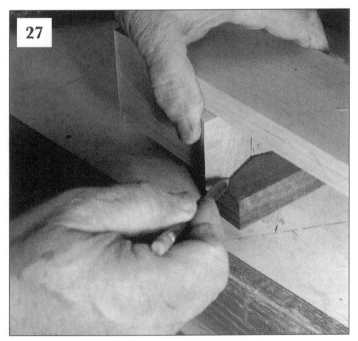

27

Mark the outer profile of the dash (10). Trace the shape of the firewall onto the dash. Cut it with the band saw.

28

Use the sanding belt to remove saw marks.

Glue the dashboard in place. Cut ⅜" from both ends to allow for the thickness of the cab sides.

Using walnut, cut the steering wheel (43) with a 1¾"-diameter hole saw. The hole saw's ¼" pilot bit makes the ¼"-diameter hole for the column (44). The column holds the wheel in place on the dash.

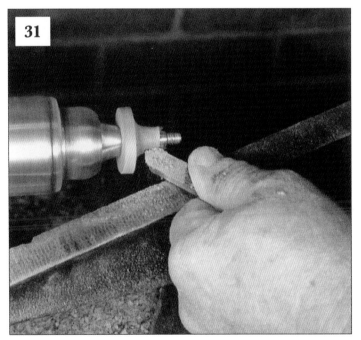

Chuck up the steering wheel on the lathe. Use a round nose scraper to shape the outer profile.

Use a skew chisel to shape the inner profile of the wheel.

Drill a hole into the dashboard for the steering wheel and column. Drill at a 30-degree angle.

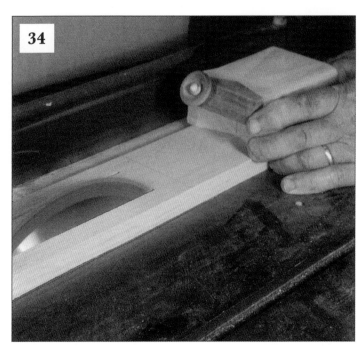

Cut away the wood on the base to make room for the wheels. Use the table saw to begin to remove the wood. (Note: The saw guard is removed for photographic purposes.)

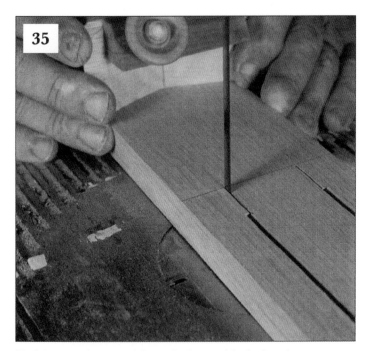

Finish removing wood from the base with the band saw.

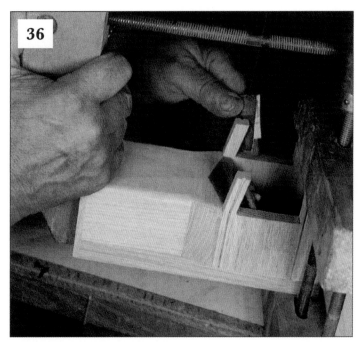

Glue and clamp the cab body in place. Make sure it is glued to both the base and the firewall.

Glue and clamp the seat (16) and seat back (15) together.

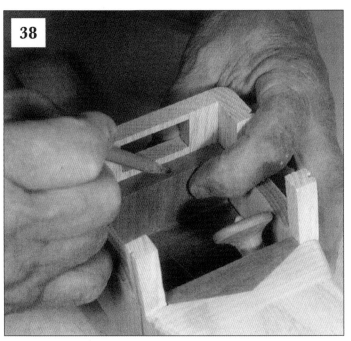

Make sure the seat assembly fits into the cab. Mark where the assembly will be sawn in half to create two seats.

Use the stationary belt sander to round the seat backs.

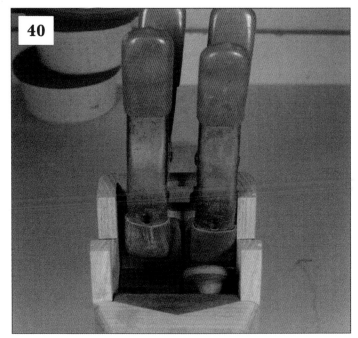

Glue and clamp the seats in place with spring clamps.

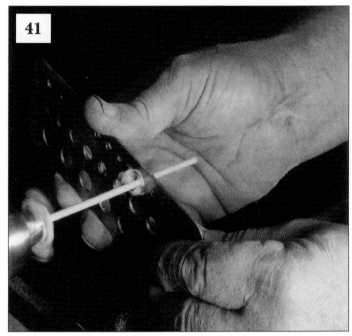

41

The windshield opening requires a vertical windshield bar (14) at its center. If you cannot find a ⅛" dowel in the wood you are using, make one using a drill bit gauge. Sharpen the edge of the steel before creating the dowel.

42

Drill the hole for the vertical bar where the dashboard meets the firewall.

43

After making the cab roof (17), which has a chevron-shaped front, measure approximately ⅛" in from the point of the front and drill a hole into the underside of the cab roof for the dowel. Trial-fit the pieces so that the roof sits snugly on the cab.

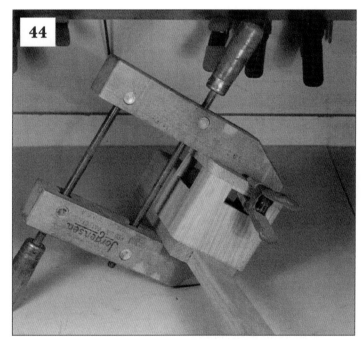

44

Glue and clamp the roof to the cab. Since you're gluing end grain to side grain, the joint will be weak. Use epoxy or reinforce the joint with small dowels or brads.

Round over the sides and back of the cab roof with the ¼" router bit.

Begin work on the oak fenders (23). To obtain the correct profile, use two hole saws, a 2½" diameter and a 3⅛" diameter. Cut partially through the inner diameter and completely through for the outer diameter.

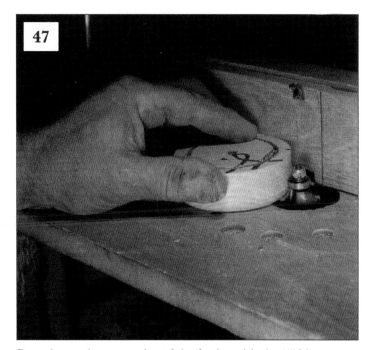

Round over the outer edge of the fender with the ¼" bit.

I fit the fender profile to a steel shaft on a stationary motor, but you could also secure to a lathe to sand the fender smooth. The pilot bit hole from the hole saw allows you to secure the fender to the shaft or a piece of metal to secure in the lathe chucks.

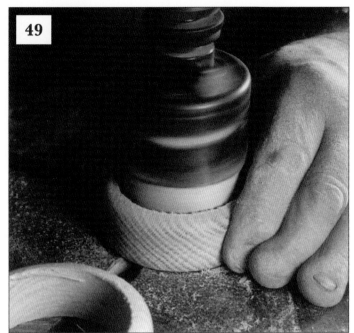

Go back to the 2½"-diameter hole saw and remove the center from the fender cutout.

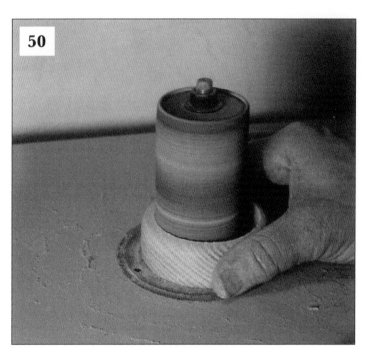

The oscillating spindle sander cleans up the inside diameter of the fender cutout.

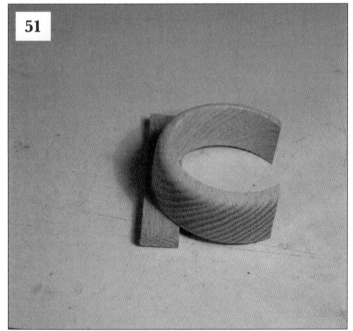

Each fender requires the addition of wood spacers (22). If you are careful, you can use the single pattern for the spacers. For a perfect fit, I make mine in two parts from ¼" x ¾" wide stock. The spacers widen the fender by ¼" and act as glue blocks so that each fender can be securely glued to the base. After cutting away part of the lower radius of the fender, glue the first spacer in place, leaving about ¼" of wood extended above the top.

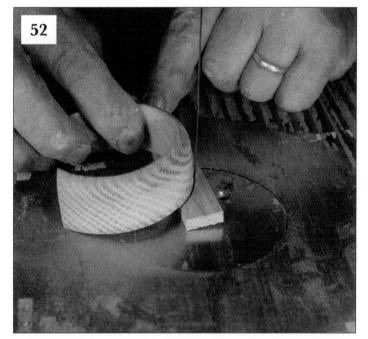

Use the band saw to cut away the excess wood of the spacer to conform to the profile of the fender cutout.

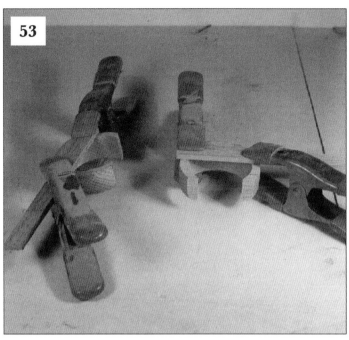

Glue the second spacer, ¼" thick by ¾" wide by at least 5" long, in place. Its width must be the same as the thickness of the base to which it will be glued.

Round over the outer edge of spacer with the ¼" bit.

Cut away more of the radius of the fender so that the front edge is lined up with the bottom of the second spacer.

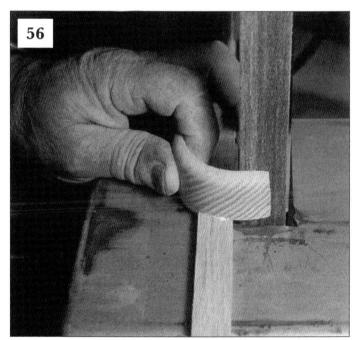

Round over the rear edge of the fender slightly.

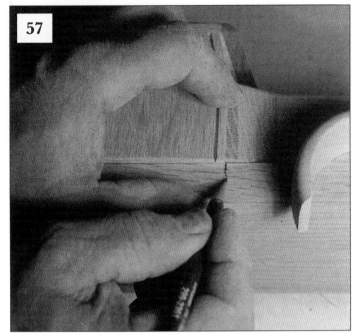

The second spacer extends only as far as the rear of the firewall. Mark the location and cut away.

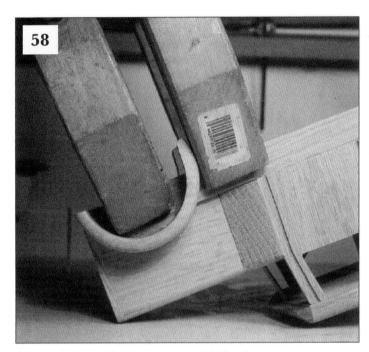

Glue and clamp the bumper assembly in place.

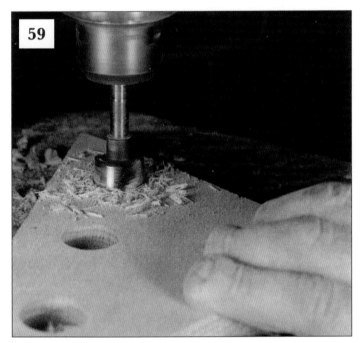

The Peterbilt truck has two different sets of wheels, all 2¼" in diameter and mounted on ⅜" dowels. The eight rear wheels (40) have a recessed front with a depth of ½". The two front wheels (39) have a flat front with grooves to represent the hubcaps. All tires facing outward have the axle holes covered with ⅜" dowel buttons. Begin with the rear wheels. Bore holes for the recesses with a 1" Forstner bit.

Drill out the entire tire circumference using a 2¼" hole saw.

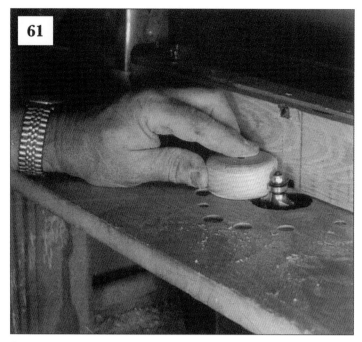

Round the edges of the tires using a ¼" roundover bit.

I fit the wheel to a steel shaft on a stationary motor, but you could also secure to a lathe to add the details to the front of the wheels.

Use a pencil compass to mark the outline of the hubcaps for the front tires.

Use a skew chisel to add the details to the front tires.

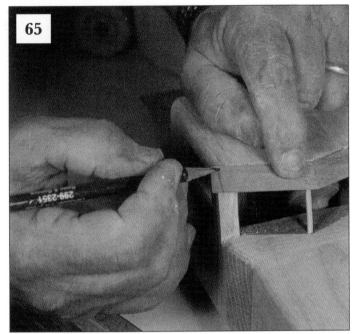

Cut the shade (18) from walnut. Fit it to the front of the cab roof and glue it in place.

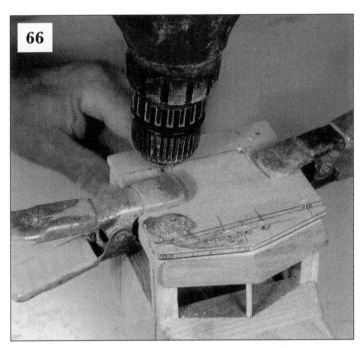

The top of the cab roof has two airhorns (42) and five clearance lamps (41). Each is mounted on a nail. I made a drilling template from scrap plywood to make it easy to drill straight holes.

Drive paneling nails (46) with the heads cut off into the holes drilled in step 66.

Only short lengths of the nails should protrude from the roof.

Drill the holes through the axle housing (6). Use a $^{27}\!/_{64}$" bit. For some, it will be easier to drill if you use a clamp to hold the blank steady.

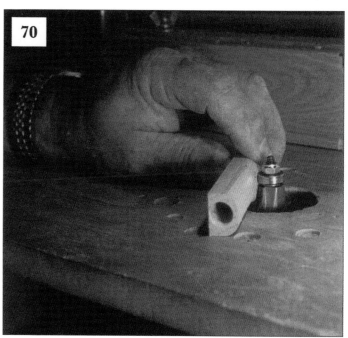

Round two edges of the axle housing with a $^{3}\!/_{8}$" bit.

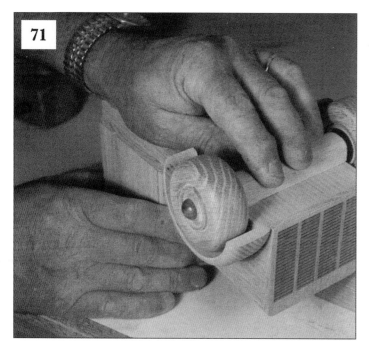

Assemble the wheels (39) and short axle (37) in the axle housing and locate its position on the base. The tires should be centered approximately $^{1}\!/_{8}$" below the fenders. If they are too far away, sand or trim the bottom of the axle housing. If they are too close, you may have to remake the axle housing using a thicker piece of wood. Do not glue the tires to the axle. Because the final step is putting a finish on the wood, you can apply the finish more easily if the tires are removed.

Mounting the rear tires requires a separate piece of wood called a rear axle housing (2). Use $^{9}\!/_{16}$" stock and drill out $^{27}\!/_{64}$" diameter holes.

PETERBILT TRUCK

The rear axle housing extends beyond the base by 5⁄16" to support the rear bumper.

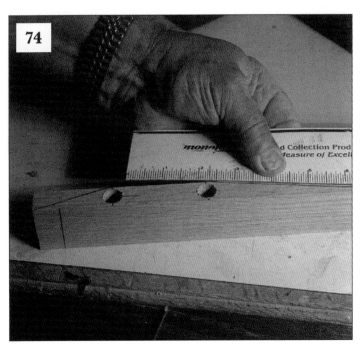

Taper the ends of the rear axle housing with the band saw.

After tapering the ends, clamp the axle housing to the base.

Assemble the wheels on the long axles (38) so that the recessed fronts are opposite each other and the unfinished backs face each other. Do not glue in place.

Check that the truck, with all tires in place, has a level body.

The rear bumper (4) does not extend beyond the outside faces of the rear tires.

Use a ⅛"-wide saw blade to cut a groove for the mud flaps (5) into the bottom of the rear bumper. Cut inner tube rubber for the mud flaps. Glue the mud flaps into the slots in the rear bumper.

Two sets of steps (29, 30) are required, one for each side of the cab. Each set of steps is the width of a door. The separation of the steps is done with a straight bit and router table or on the table saw. Or, two pieces of wood can be glued together to make the steps. A rabbet is then cut into the top rear of the steps. The bottom edge of the base in front of the doors will fit into the rabbet.

PETERBILT TRUCK

The steps are cut to length quickly on a radial arm saw. (Note: The saw guard is removed for photographic purposes.)

Drill holes into the rabbet and into the truck base so the two can be joined with paneling nails.

Once the steps are fixed onto the nails, they are glued in place.

Air tanks (31) for the brakes are fitted into the space between the top of the steps and the bottom of the door. The space available should be ½". Mounted on each side, these are half cylinders that have grooves ½" in from either side. Sandwich the dowel between stop blocks and rotate the dowel against the band saw blade to cut the grooves.

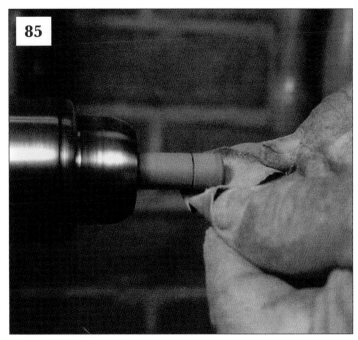

Put the tanks into a lathe drill chuck and round the ends slightly. The tanks are flattened to three-quarters of their thickness on the stationary belt sander.

Fit the tanks in place. They are only as wide as the doors.

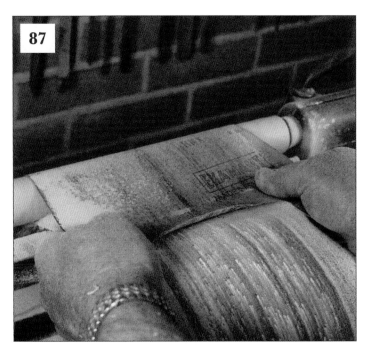

Two gas tanks (32) are required, one for each side of the cab. Each is 1⁵⁄₁₆" in diameter. If a dowel is not available, turn your wood on the lathe. A wide sanding belt quickly removes tool marks on the turning wood.

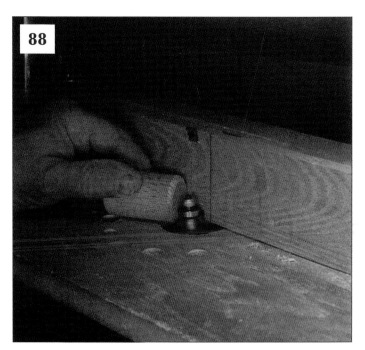

The ends of the tanks must be rounded. Rotate the tanks against a ⅛" roundover bit.

Each tank has two ³⁄₁₆" strips of wood around its circumference to represent mounting straps. If veneer is not available, run narrow strips through a thickness planer to get the wood as thin as possible.

To get the strips even thinner, run the strips between a sanding disc and a board clamped a veneer-width away from the edge of the disc where it is turning into the table.

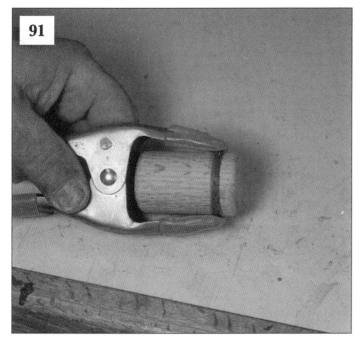

Glue and clamp the strips to the air tanks.

Clamp the tanks between the lathe centers and waste wood to sand the strips and give them a slightly rounded contour.

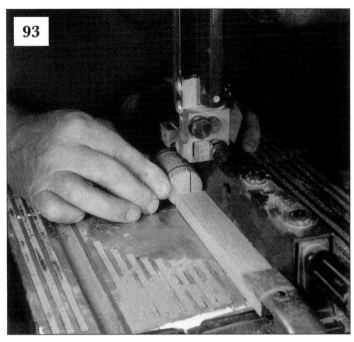

Each tank must have a corner removed so it can rest flush to the base. Use a band saw and stop block to cut away the wood.

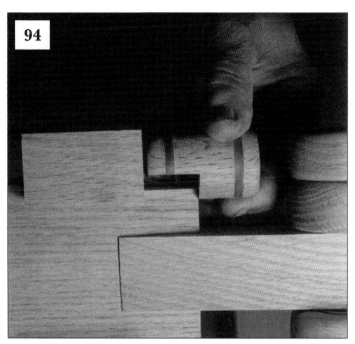

The tanks are held in place with paneling nails and glue.

Behind the cab is a base plate (19). Made from ⅛" stock, it is as wide as the cab.

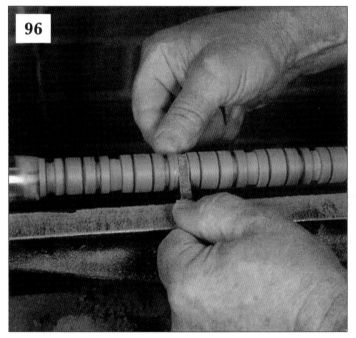

Two air cleaners (33) are required. Made of contrasting wood and ⅞" in diameter, the air cleaners have a variety of grooves that are cut on the lathe. If you are making more than one truck at a time, it is wise to make multiples of accessories like air cleaners and fuel tanks.

PETERBILT TRUCK

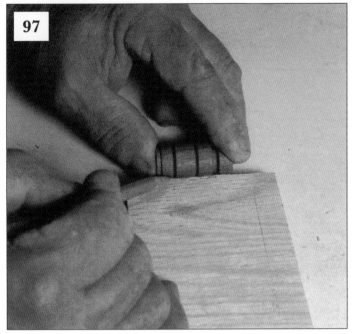

The air cleaners are mounted to the sides of the firewall using paneling nails. To line up the nail holes perfectly, use a board one-half the diameter of the tanks and mark where you want to drill the holes.

Mount the air cleaners. Make sure to remove the heads of the nails and hammer gently.

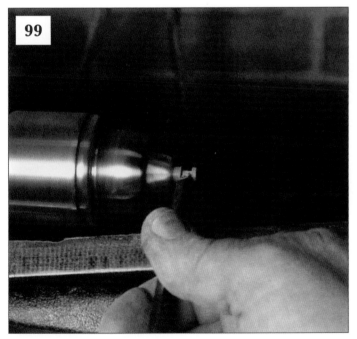

The radiator cap is made from ¼"-diameter contrasting wood. Turn its shape on the lathe.

Each fuel tank has a ¼"-diameter gas cap glued in place.

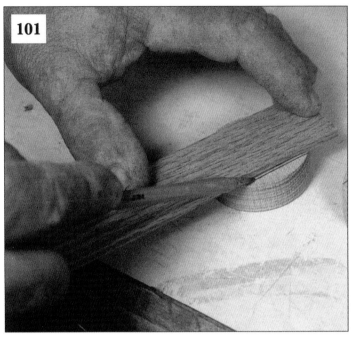

The hitch wheel (21) is mounted on the rear of the truck. It has a ½"-diameter hole to accept the trailer dowel hitch. The wheel, 2" in diameter, has a ¼"-wide rabbet removed from its underside. The inside edges of the rabbet must line up with the width of the base and rear axle housing.

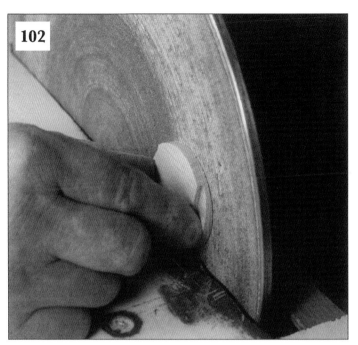

Add a 5-degree taper to the top of the hitch wheel. Use the sanding disc. After gluing the hitch disc in place, drill a ½"-diameter by 1"-deep hole through the wheel into the base and rear axle housing.

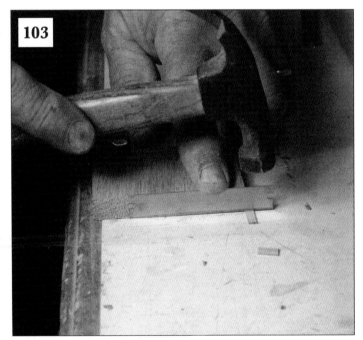

The front bumper (7) is made of contrasting wood, while areas that represent rectangular and round holes are made from the same wood as the body. The veneer-thin pieces are cut to size with a scalpel or a razor blade.

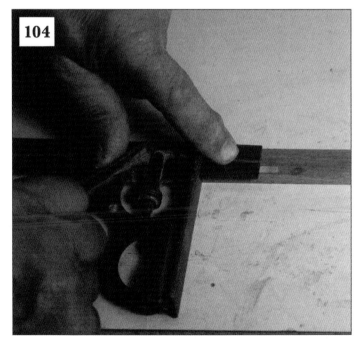

Use a combination square to space the "holes" an equal distance from the ends of the bumper.

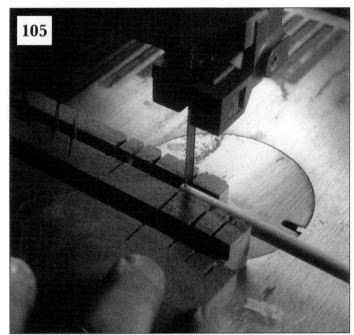

Use a dowel-holding fixture to cut the "holes" as thinly as possible.

The bumper is held in place with a bumper support (3) glued to the underside of the base.

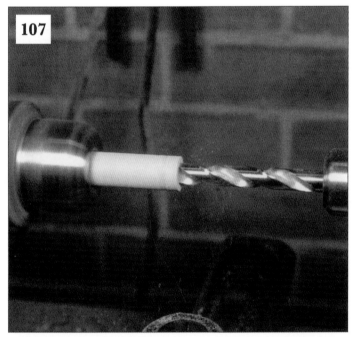

Two stacks (20) are required for the rear of the cab. They can be made from two separate pieces of wood, ⅜" and ⅝" in diameter, and fitted into one another. Alternately, they can be turned as a single unit on the lathe. If made from two separate pieces, secure the larger diameter dowel in a lathe drill chuck and bore a hole.

The stacks are held in place with paneling nails. Use a hammer and scrap wood to fit them onto the nails.

The truck has three oval emblems: one for the front, two for the sides of the hood. Using needle-nose pliers to hold a thin piece of walnut that measures ¼" by ½", sand the corners of the wood lightly to give them a slightly rounded appearance.

Work on the cab roof lamps (41) and airhorns (42) using contrasting wood. If you do not have the correct diameter dowel, you can start with an oversized dowel and reduce it using a drill gauge.

Use a dowel-holding fixture to drill the holes for the paneling nails that hold the lights to the roof.

The drill gauge used to resize dowels works as a sanding fixture. Hold a light in the appropriate hole and push the gauge along a flat sheet of sandpaper. The elliptical back of the light is done by holding the dowel at an angle to a belt sander or disc sander and rotating it before cutting it to size.

Mount the lights onto the paneling nails.

The airhorns are turned on a lathe using ½"-diameter contrasting wood dowels. Use a round nose scraper to hollow out the front of the horn.

Use a parting tool to shape the rear of the airhorn.

Mount the airhorns on the paneling nails.

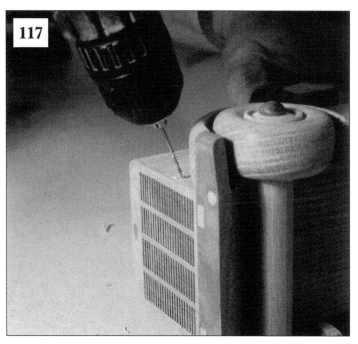

Two sets of headlights (35) and supports (34) are required for the front of the truck. Mounted with paneling nails on both sides of the hood, the frames have contrasting wood lights ⅜" in diameter.

Cut out and glue in place veneer-thin pieces for the door handles.

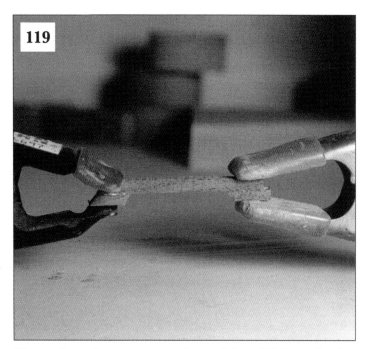

The truck requires two contrasting grab bars (12) for each side of the cab. An easy way to make them is to glue up separate pieces to form the shape of the bars.

Use a sanding stick to round the grab bars.

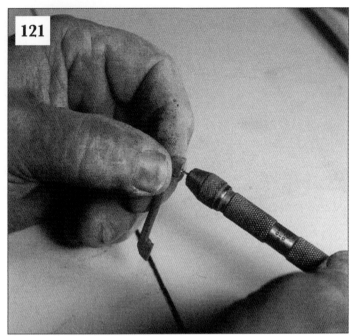

Attach the grab bars with paneling nails. Use a pin vise to drill the holes for the nails.

Gently tap the handles in place.

Begin work on the trailer. The trailer is basically a box with two sides (3), a top or roof (4), a base or floor (1), a front (2), and a sliding door (20, 21) at the rear. The roof, floor, and sides are made from ½" stock. Cut a ½"-wide by ¼"-deep dado into the floor of the trailer. Once the trailer is completed, you can move on to the doors.

The trailer has a tambour door. Furniture tambours are slats with canvas backing. Use a beveled cabinet tambour with ¼"-thick by ¾"-wide slats. (See page 109 for information about sourcing a tambour.) Each slat, with the exception of the bottom one, is cut in half lengthwise. Use the radial arm saw, but do not cut through the canvas. (Note: The saw guard was removed for photographic purposes.)

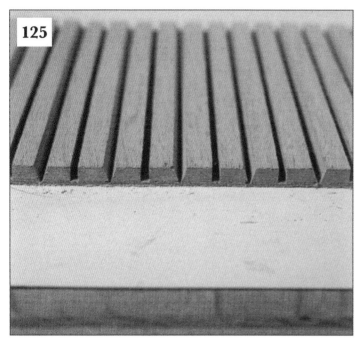

Here is a profile of the tambour after crosscutting each slat. An alternative is to make your own tambour. (See page 109 for information about an article that can help you learn to do this.)

Both sides of the cab have grooves that represent aluminum siding. Each cut is ½" apart on center using a ⅛"-wide saw blade.

A vertical track is made on the rear ends of the trailer sides; a horizontal track is made along the trailer sides in which the tambour door will move. The horizontal track does not extend the entire length of the trailer but only so far as to allow the door to ride up until it reaches its bottom slat at the top of the door opening.

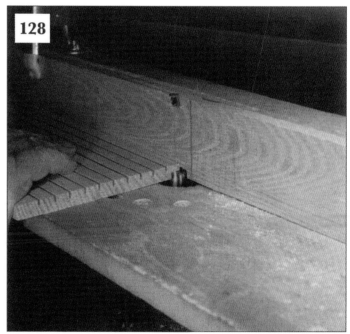

Use a straight bit and router table to cut the track slots.

A sanding stick, which is sandpaper glued to a board, rounds over the corner of the track for the tambour door. This enables the door to ride smoothly up into the slot.

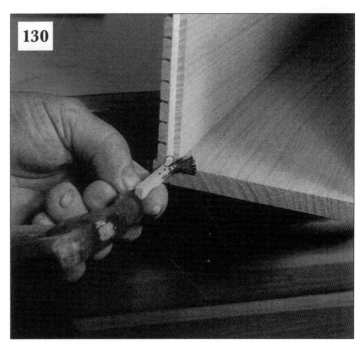

Assemble the sides and floor, then glue. Because the vertical tracks for the tambour door leave gaps where the sides meet the floor, the gaps must be filled with strips of wood and the excess trimmed away.

Fit the front support (2a) between the sides in the front of the trailer. This piece, not shown in the drawings, stiffens the assembly, keeps the sides parallel, and provides a glue surface for the front panel.

Cut the front panel to size, route its edges with a ¼" roundover bit, and glue it in place.

The tambour door is held in place on the bottom by the bumper (5). Glue and clamp the bumper in place.

Clamp the top (4) of the trailer in place.

Round over the top edges using a ¼" roundover bit and router table.

Cut the tambour door to size and make sure it slides up and down freely.

PETERBILT TRUCK

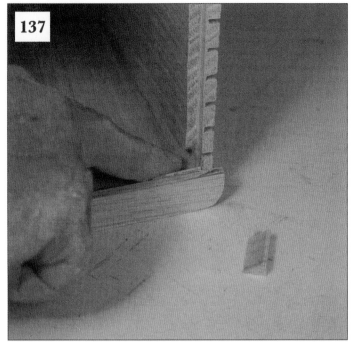

Glue beveled stops made from scrap wood in place on the underside of the roof to help keep the tambour door from binding where the roof meets the doorframe.

Lock the door in place on the sides with the door spacers (21a). These pieces, not shown in the drawings, help the door slide smoothly. Since you are gluing end grain to side grain, use epoxy.

The door handle (25) consists of a veneer-thin piece of contrasting wood.

Cut the axle housing (6) to size and drill $^{27}\!/_{64}$"-diameter holes 2½" apart for the axles.

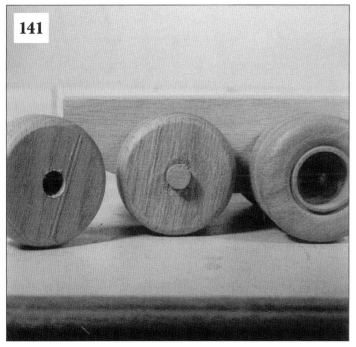

Four pairs of wheels (25) are required, plus two spares. Each has a 1"-diameter by ½"-deep hole cut into its center. Each tire is shaped and detailed. (See steps 59–62, pages 48–49, for making the rear wheels of the truck.)

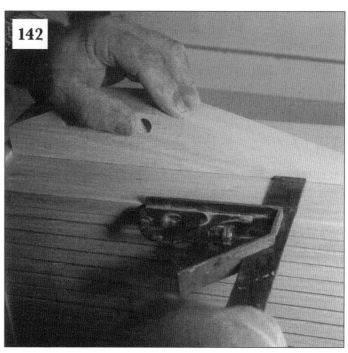

Use a combination square to center the axle housing.

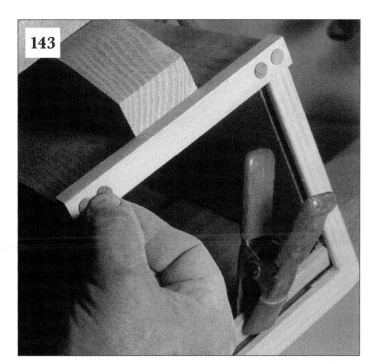

After gluing the axle housing in place, cut the rear trailer frame top (19) and sides (26). Cut out four contrasting wood lights from a ⁵⁄₁₆" dowel and glue them in place.

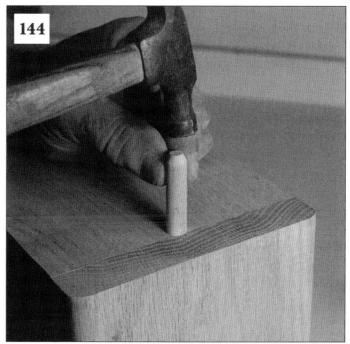

The trailer hitch (12) consists of a ⁷⁄₁₆"-diameter dowel.

The legs (13) or dolly, which supports the trailer when it stands apart from the truck, is made from ⅜"-square stock. The leg ends are turned round so that they will fit into holes drilled into the floor of the trailer.

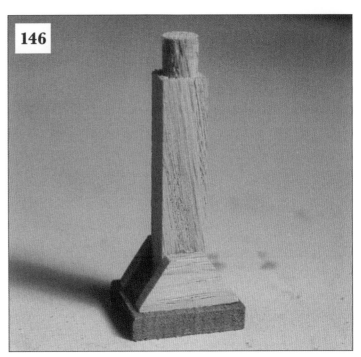

Glue and clamp the bottom braces (15) and contrasting wood foot (17) onto each leg.

The legs are connected by a bar (14) made from a ⅛" dowel. Once you have located the position of the legs, determine the length of the bar.

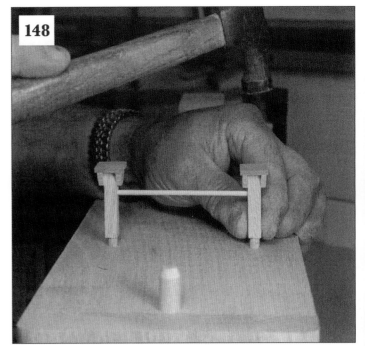

Gently tap the legs and connecting bar in place on the underside of the floor.

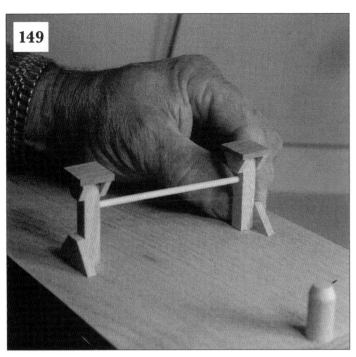

The legs have top braces (15) that help secure the legs to the underside of the floor.

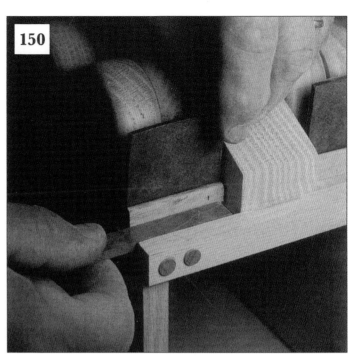

Make mud flap holders (10) using ⅜"-wide stock. The mud flaps (11) are made from inner tube rubber. Use a spacer to place them parallel to the rear edge of the trailer. The mud flaps are held in place using paneling nails and glue.

Assemble the rear bumper extension (8) and stop (9) using contrasting wood.

Glue the bumper extension assembly in place to the rear of the axle housing.

PETERBILT TRUCK

The last woodworking step is to mount the spare tires. Use ⅜" dowels to hold them in place.

Dip the truck and trailer into a finishing oil. If the tires and other accessories (such as airhorns) are removed before dipping, they can be finished separately in smaller containers.

If the container is not big enough for dipping, pour the finishing oil over the truck and trailer. After the first application has dried, dip and pour a second application. Then rub the truck with a finishing cloth.

ADDITIONAL PROJECTS

The classic form of the Ford Model A Pickup works well in wood—be it the swooping curve of the fenders or the squared bed below. Turn the page for more photos. See page 90 for the measured drawings.

The 1932 Buick Sedan is another classic that you'll enjoy carving.

See page 77 for the measured drawings.

Veneer trim is used extensively on a Sam Martin piece—even on this flatbed trailer. The flatbed trailer can be pulled by the same truck design as the van trailer found earlier in this book (page 28). See page 103 for the measured drawings.

1932 Buick Sedan Parts List

Piece #	Piece	Size (inches)	Quantity
1	Base	¾ × 4 × 11⅜	1
2	Support	⅜ Dia. × ¾	4
3	Bumper	⅝ × ⅝ × 6¼	2
4	Hood	2¼ × 3⅝ × 3	1
5	Cowl	⅞ × 2¼ × 4	1
6	Side	¼ x ⅞ x 1½	2
7	Side	¼ x 1½ x 1½	2
8	Side	¼ x ¾ x 1½	2
9	Radiator Frame	3/16 × 1⅞ × 2¾	1
10	Radiator	3/16 × 1½ × 2⅜	1
11	Trim	⅛ × 1⅞ × 2¾	1
12	Side	⅜ × 3 7/16 × 6⅝	2
13	Front	⅜ × 2 7/16 × 3¼	1
14	Back	⅜ × 3¼ × 3 7/16	1
15	Dash	¾ × 11/16 × 3¼	1
16	Support	⅛ × 2¼ × 3¼	2
17	Steering Wheel	1½ Dia. × 13/16	1
18	Column	¼ Dia. × 1½	1
19	Fender	1 × 2 × 11⅞	2
20	Spacer	⅜ × 1⅜ × 3⅞	2
21	Stop Light	7/16 Dia. × 13/16	2
22	Support	⅛ Dia. × 4¼	1
23	Light	11/16 Dia. × 11/16	2
24	Paneling Nails	1/16 × ¾	As Required
25	Cap	5/16 Dia. × ⅝	1
26	Riser	½ × 1¼ × 3⅛	1
27	Seat	¼ × 1¼ × 3⅛	2
28	Roof	¾ × 4 × 7	1
29	Axle	⅜ Dia. × 6	2
30	Wheel	2⅜ Dia. × 15/16	5
31	Axle	⅜ Dia. × 2	1
32	Cap	⅜ Dia. Dowel Button	5

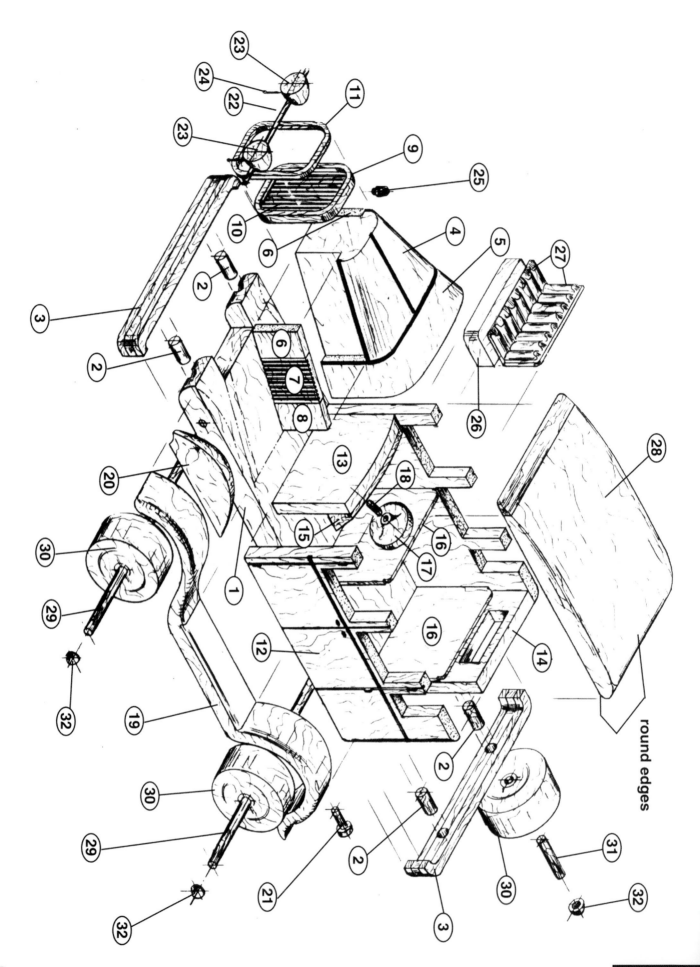

round edges

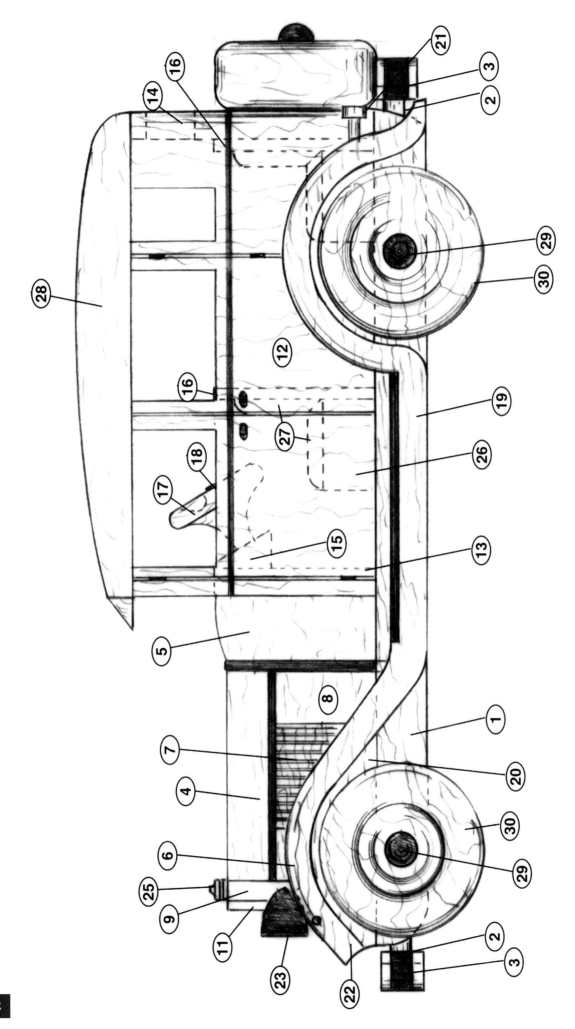

1932 BUICK SEDAN

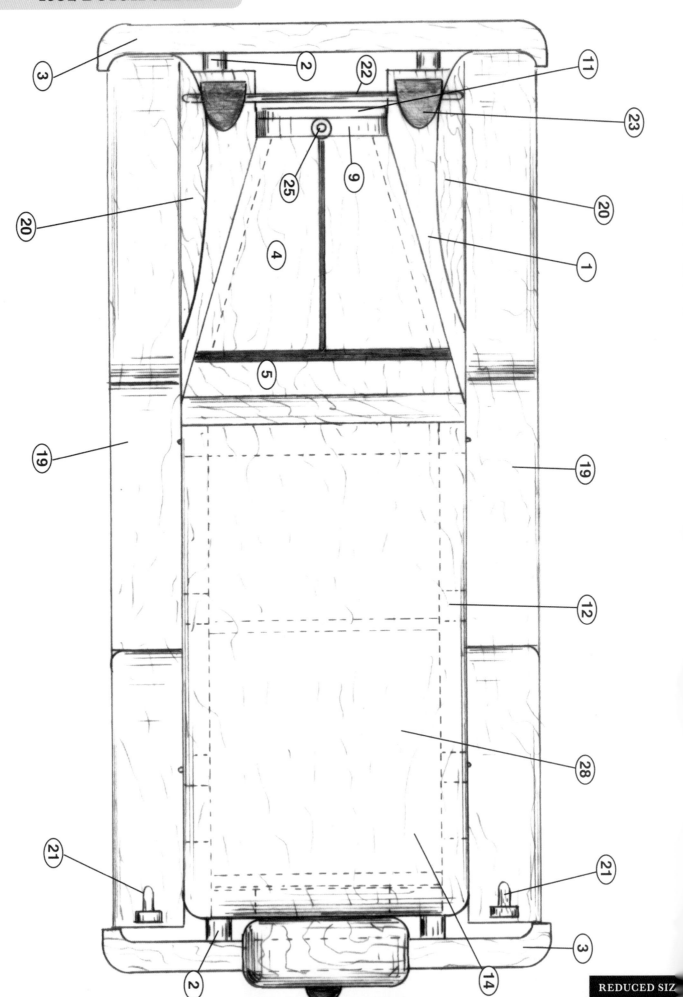

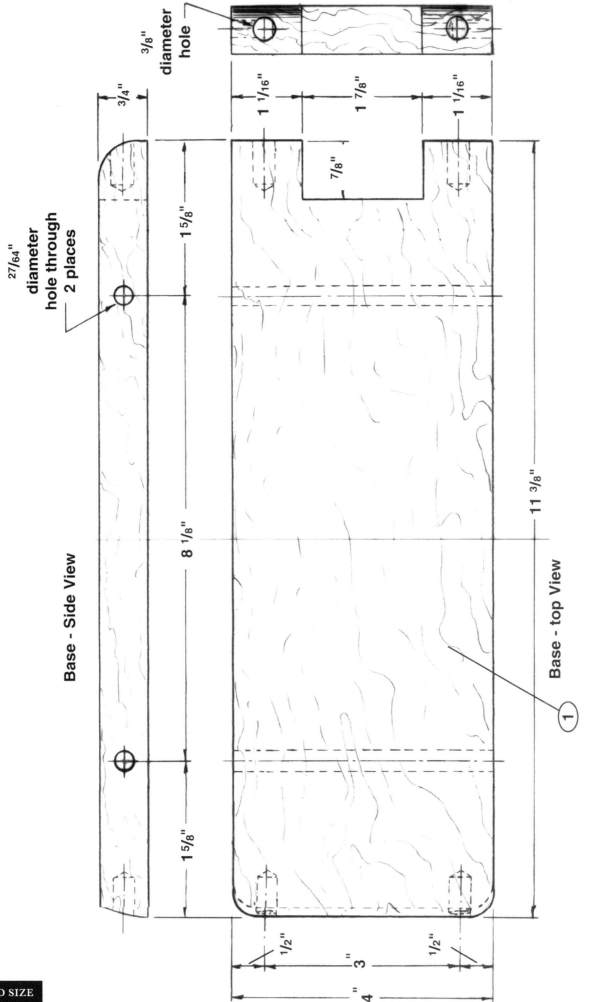

3/8" diameter hole

3/4"

1 1/16"

1 7/8"

1 1/16"

7/8"

27/64" diameter hole through 2 places

1 5/8"

8 1/8"

11 3/8"

Base - Side View

1 5/8"

1/2"

3"

1/2"

4"

Base - top View

1

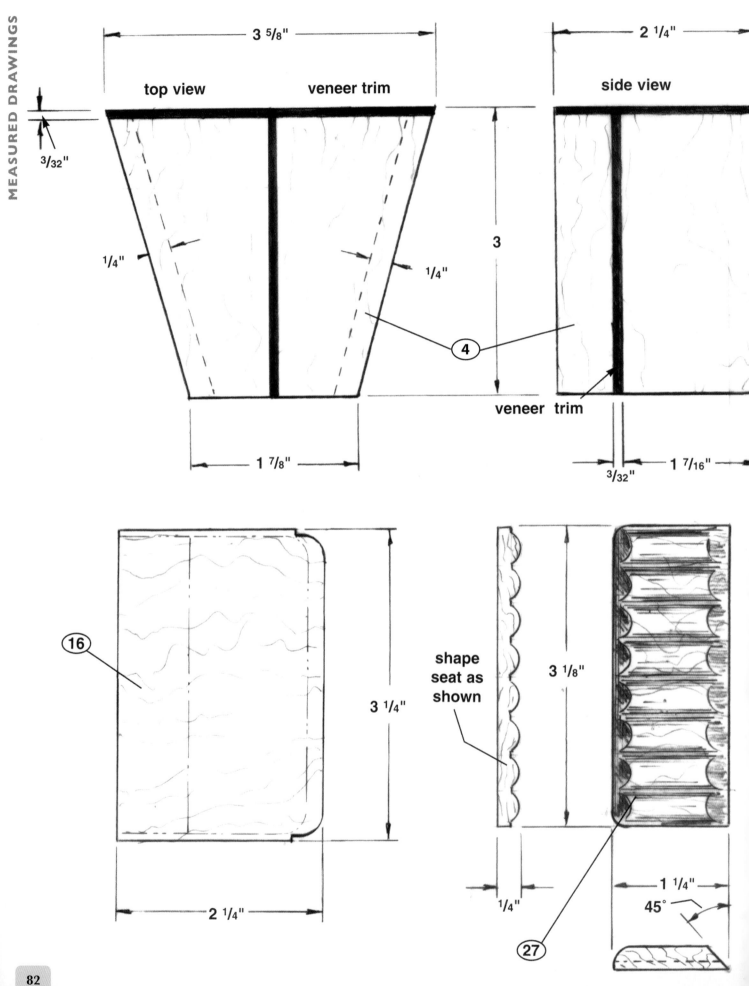

top view   veneer trim

side view

3 5/8"

2 1/4"

3/32"

1/4"

1/4"

3

4

veneer trim

1 7/8"

3/32"

1 7/16"

16

shape
seat as
shown

3 1/8"

3 1/4"

3 1/4"

2 1/4"

1/4"

1 1/4"

45°

27

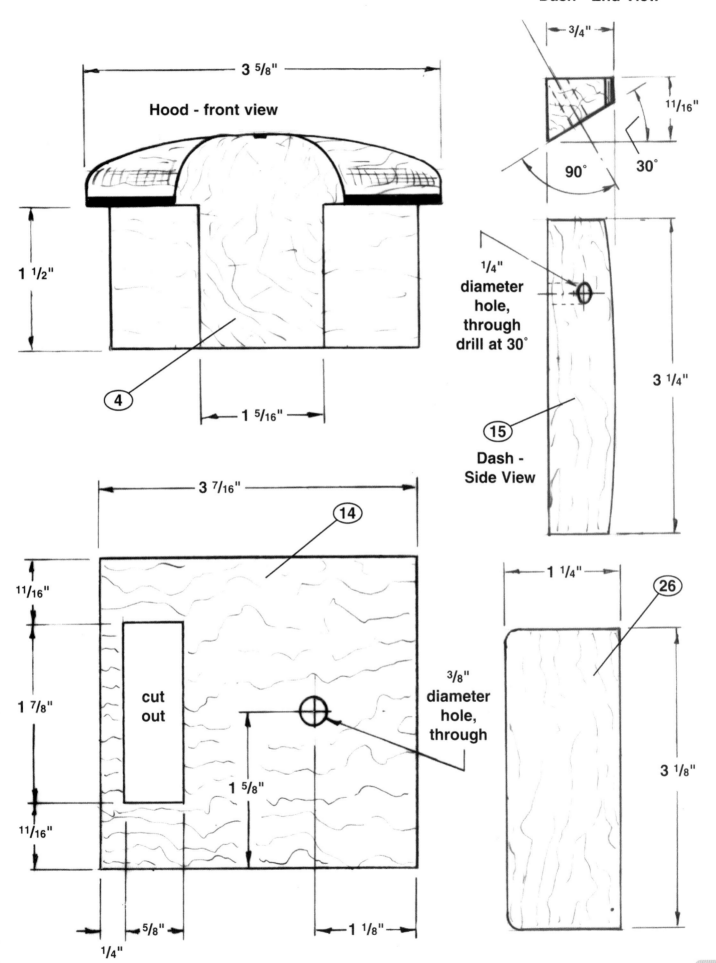

Dash - End View

3/4"

11/16"

90°   30°

3 5/8"

Hood - front view

1 1/2"

④

1 5/16"

¼"
diameter
hole,
through
drill at 30°

3 1/4"

⑮

**Dash -
Side View**

3 7/16"

⑭

11/16"

1 7/8"

cut
out

3/8"
diameter
hole,
through

1 5/8"

5/8"

¼"

1 1/8"

1 1/4"

㉖

3 1/8"

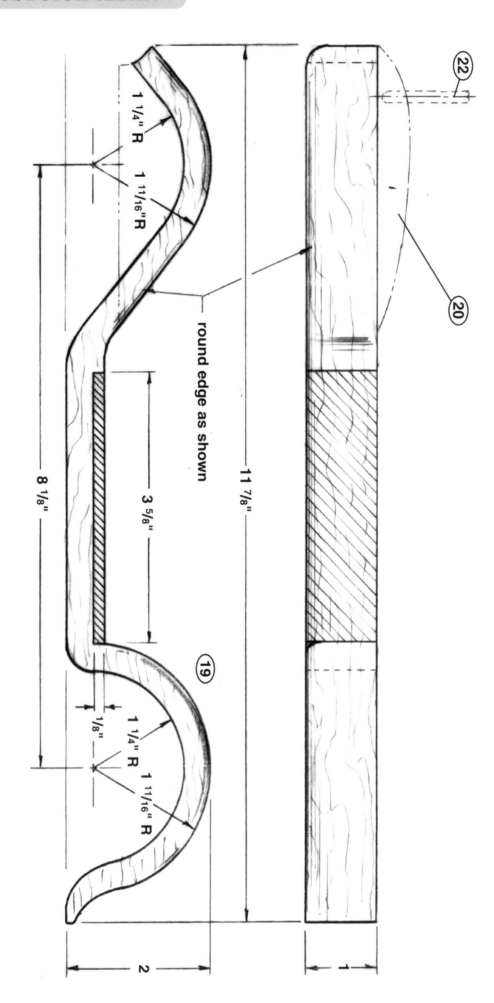

1 1/4" R

1 11/16" R

round edge as shown

11 7/8"

8 1/8"

3 5/8"

19

1/8"

1 1/4" R

1 11/16" R

22

20

2

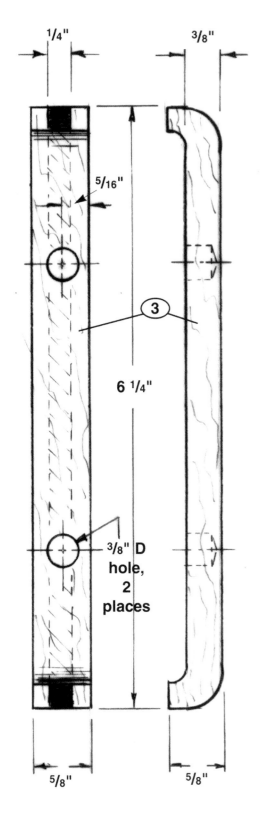

1/4"

3/8"

5/16"

③

6 1/4"

3/8" D hole, 2 places

5/8"

5/8"

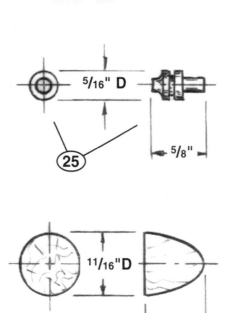

5/16" D

25

5/8"

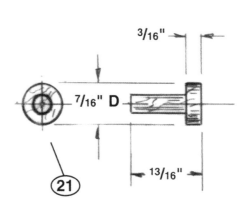

11/16" D

23

11/16"

3/16"

7/16" D

21

13/16"

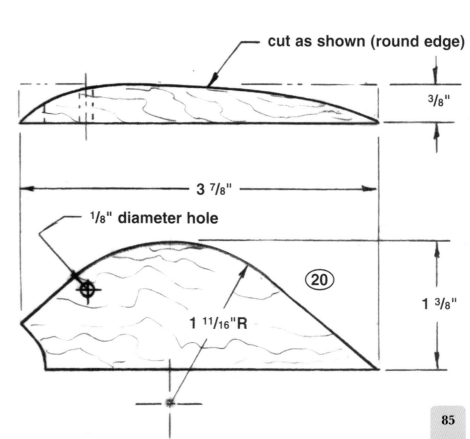

cut as shown (round edge)

3/8"

3 7/8"

1/8" diameter hole

20

1 3/8"

1 11/16" R

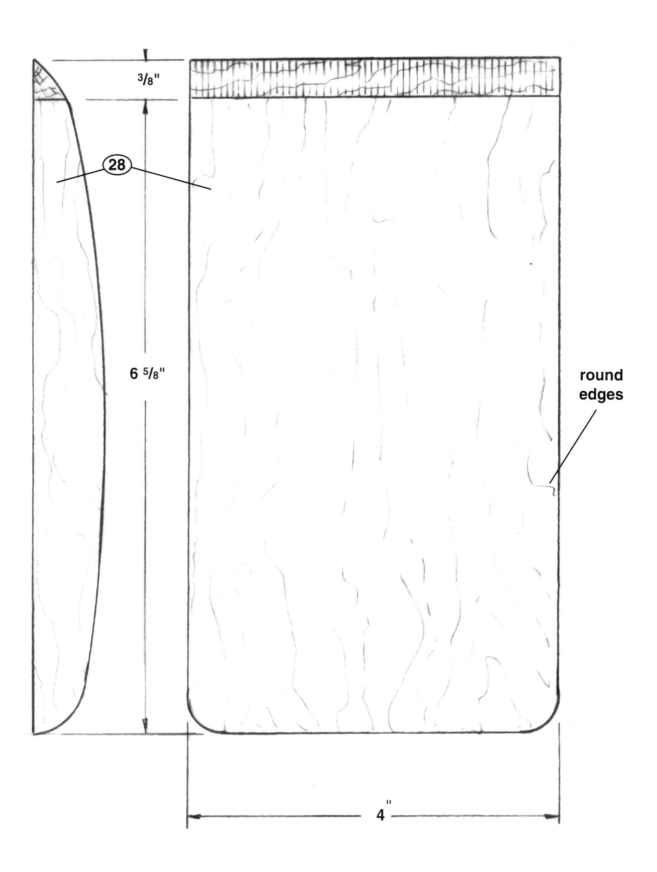

3/8"

28

6 5/8"

round
edges

4"

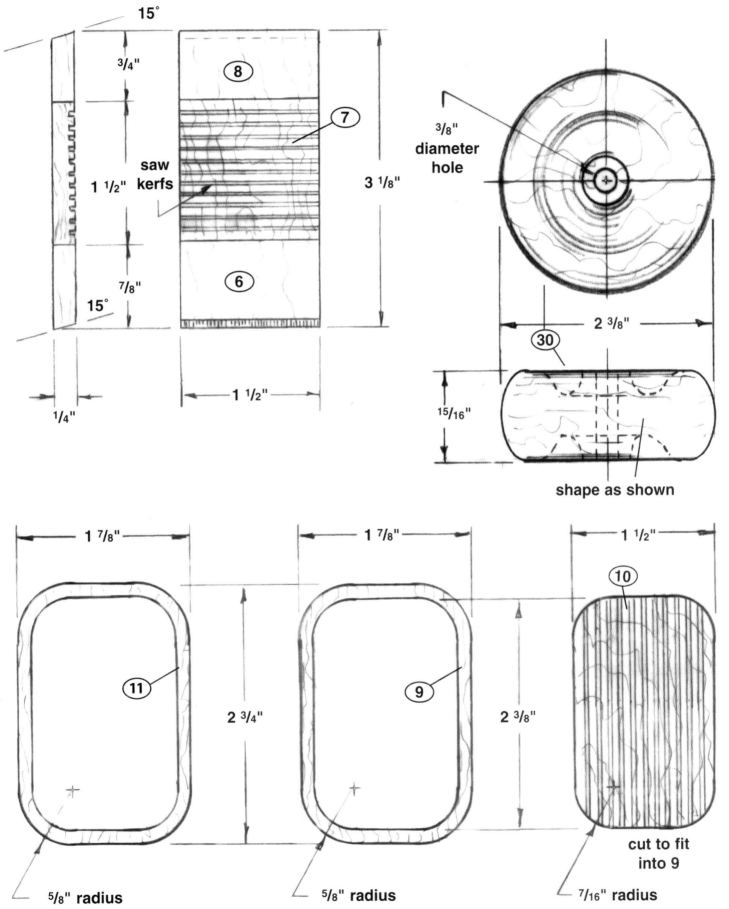

15°

3/4"

8

7

saw
kerfs

1 1/2"

7/8"

6

15°

3 1/8"

1/4"

1 1/2"

3/8"
diameter
hole

2 3/8"

30

15/16"

shape as shown

1 7/8"

1 7/8"

1 1/2"

10

11

9

2 3/4"

2 3/8"

cut to fit
into 9

5/8" radius

5/8" radius

7/16" radius

87

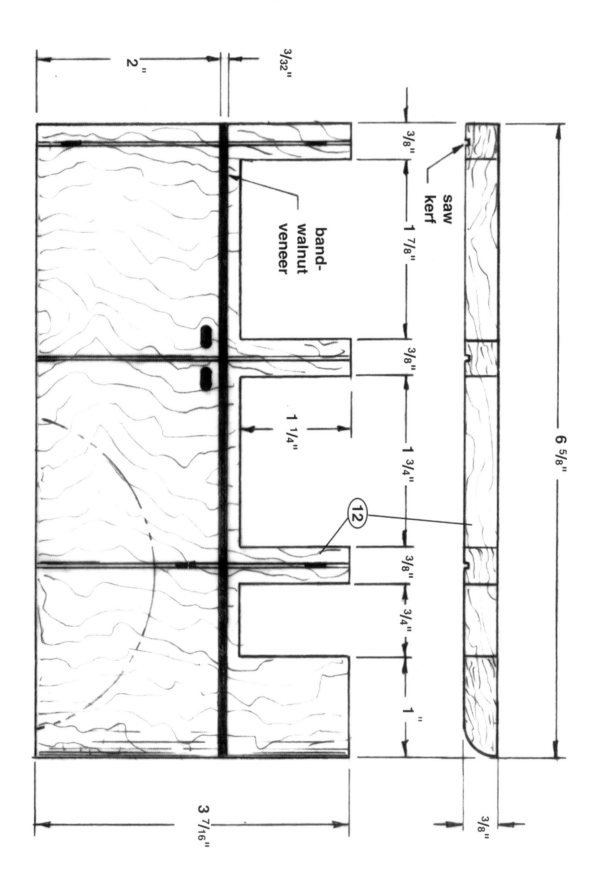

band-
walnut
veneer

saw
kerf

2"

3/32"

3/8"

1 7/8"

3/8"

1 1/4"

1 3/4"

3/8"

3/4"

1"

6 5/8"

3/8"

3 7/16"

(12)

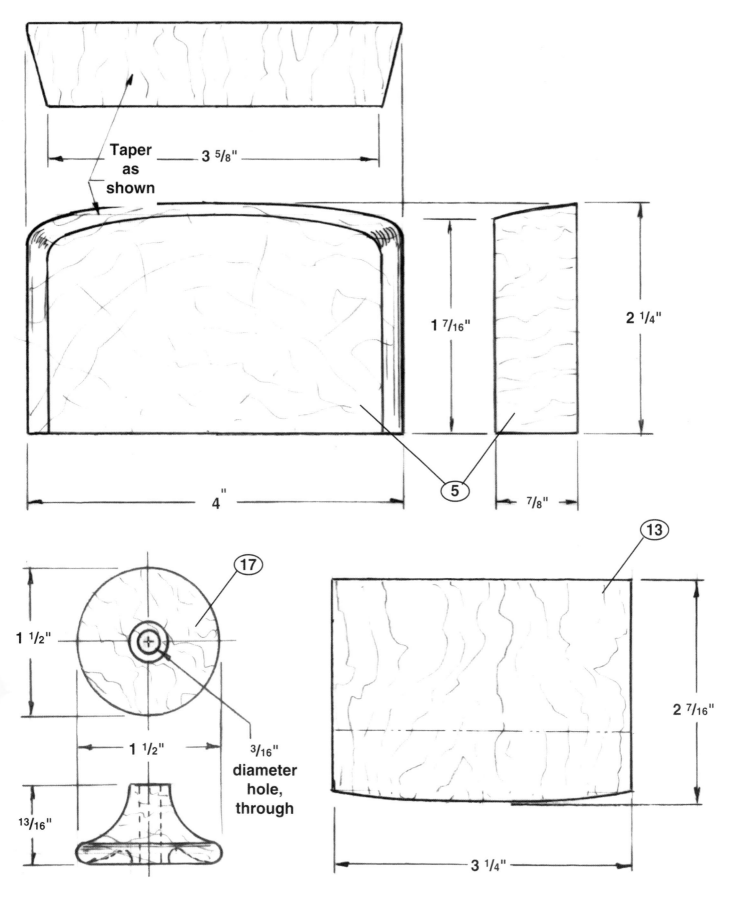

Taper as shown

3 ⁵/₈"

1 ⁷/₁₆"

2 ¹/₄"

4"

5

⁷/₈"

13

1 ¹/₂"

17

¹³/₁₆"

1 ¹/₂"

³/₁₆" diameter hole, through

2 ⁷/₁₆"

3 ¹/₄"

Ford Model A Pickup Parts List

PIECE #	PIECE	SIZE (INCHES)	QUANTITY
1	Base	¾ × 3⅝ × 11⅞	1
2	Support	⅜ Dia. × Length To Fit	2
3	Bumper	⅝ × ⅝ × 6	1
4	Hood	1⅝ × 3¼ × 2¾	1
5	Trim	¼ × 1⅛ × ¹¹⁄₁₆	2
6	Trim	¼ × 1⅛ × 1½	2
7	Trim	¼ × 1⅛ × ¹³⁄₁₆	2
8	Cowl (Front)	⅛ × 1 ¹³⁄₁₆ × 2¾	1
9	Cowl (Back)	⅛ × 1 ¹³⁄₁₆ × 2¾	1
10	Radiator	⅛ × 1⁹⁄₁₆ × 1 ¹⁵⁄₁₆	1
11	Cap	⁵⁄₁₆ Dia. × ⅝	1
12	Cowl (Back)	1¾ × 3¼ × 3½	1
13	Door	⅜ × 2⅞ × 2 ¹⁵⁄₁₆	2
14	Front (Cab)	⅜ × 1⅝ × 2¾	1
15	Dash	⅝ × ¾ × 2¾	1
16	Back (Cab)	⅜ × 1⅝ × 2¾	1
17	Riser	½ × 1¼ × 2¾	1
18	Seat	¼ × 1¼ 2¾	2
19	Steering Wheel	1½ Dia. × ¹³⁄₁₆	1
20	Column	¼ Dia. × 1½	1
21	Cap (Back)	⅞ × 1¼ × 3½	1
22	Running Board	¹⁵⁄₁₆ × 2⅛ × 13	2
23	Spacer	⅛ × 1⅜ × 3⅝	2
24	Spacer	⁷⁄₁₆ × 1⅜ × 3⅜	2
25	Stop Light	⁷⁄₁₆ Dia. × ¾	1
26	Light Support	⅛ Dia. × 4⅜	1
27	Headlight	¾ Dia. × ½	2
28	Paneling Nails	Small	2
29	Roof	⁹⁄₁₆ × 3¼ × 3½	1
30	Bed	⅜ × 3 × 4½	1
31	Ends	⅜ × 1¼ × 3	2
32	Side	⅜ × 1¼ × 5	2
33	Lip	¼ × ⅝ × 5	2
34	Trim	¹⁄₃₂ × ¼ × 1	6
35	Trim	¹⁄₃₂ × ¼ × 5	2
36	Trim	¹⁄₃₂ × ¼ × 3	1
37	Axle	¼ Dia. × 1½	4
38	Wheel	2⅜ Dia. × ¹⁵⁄₁₆	4
39	Milk Can	⅞ Dia. × 1 ¹³⁄₁₆	6
40	Cap	¼ Dia. Dowel Button	4

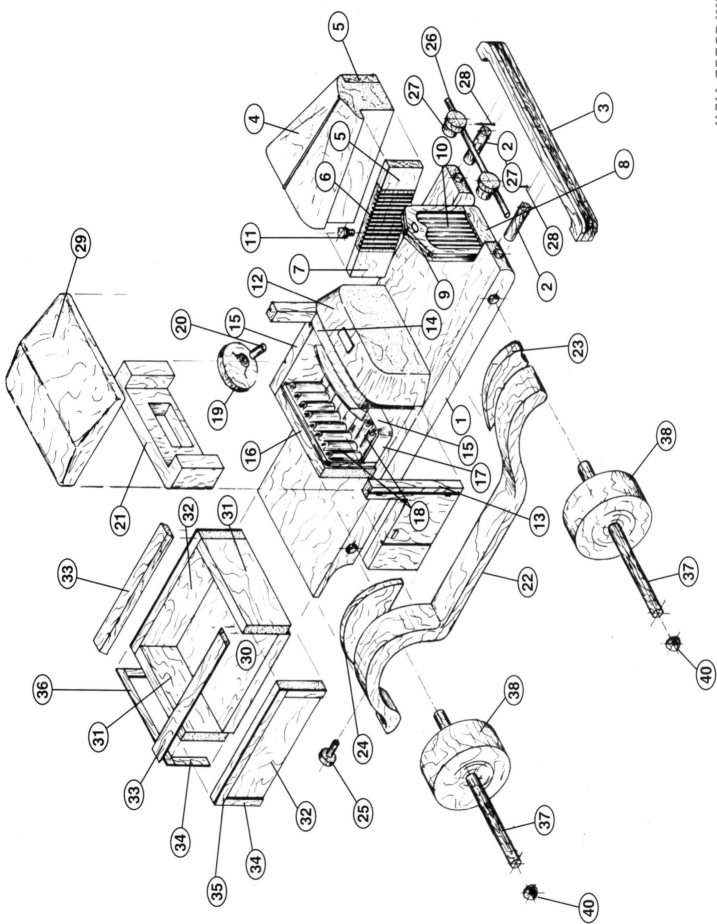

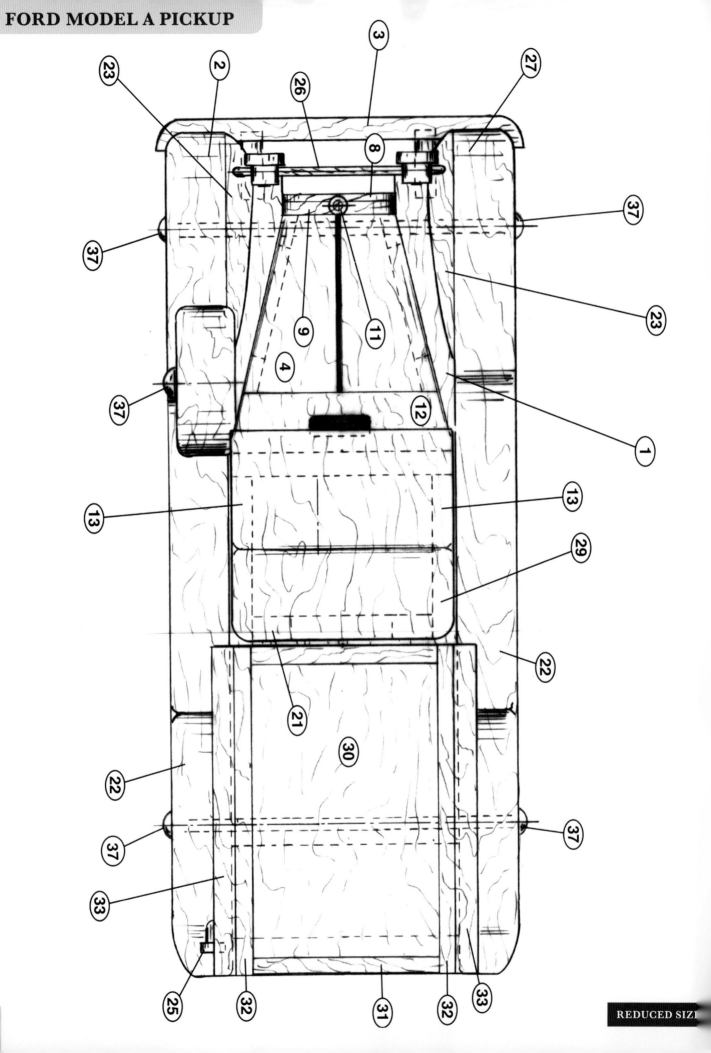

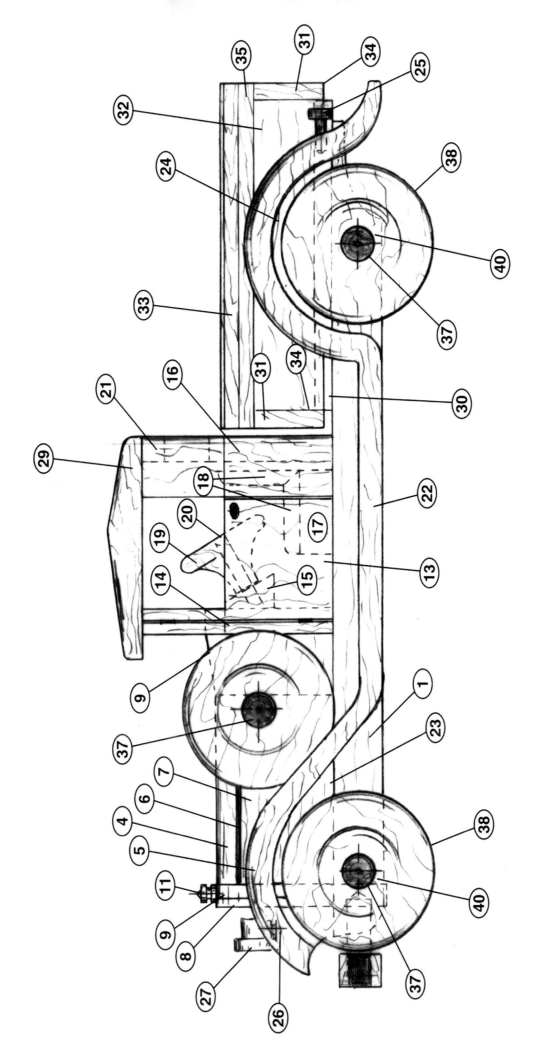

FORD MODEL A PICKUP

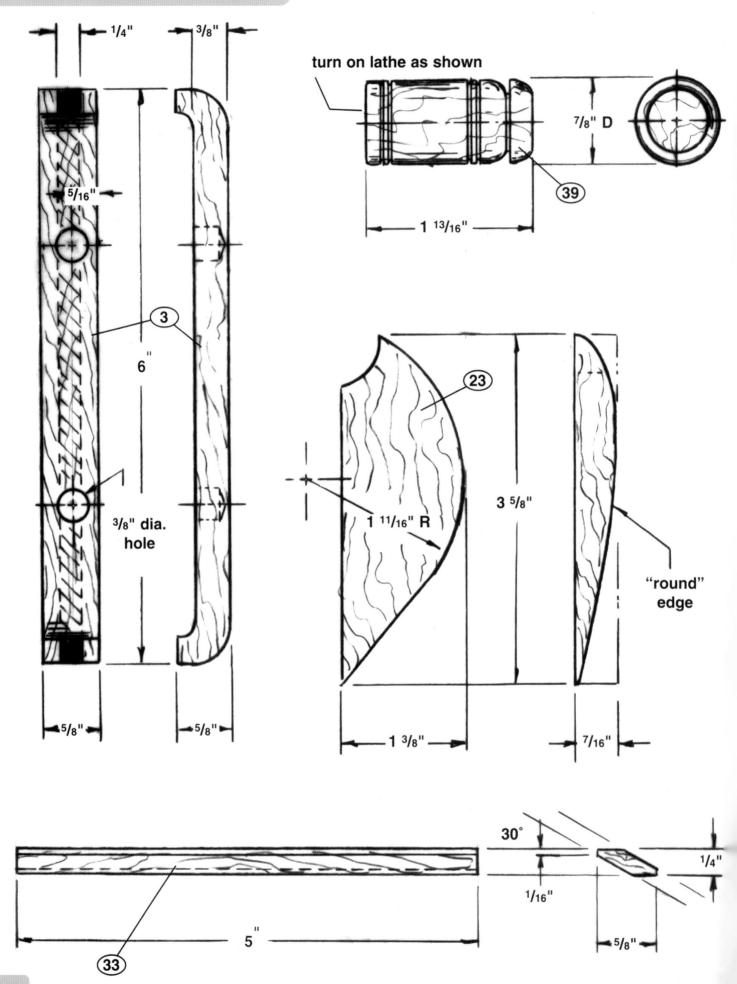

1/4" 3/8"

turn on lathe as shown

7/8" D

1 13/16"

39

5/16"

3

6"

3/8" dia.
hole

5/8" 5/8"

23

1 11/16" R

3 5/8"

"round"
edge

1 3/8" 7/16"

30°

1/4"

1/16"

5"

5/8"

33

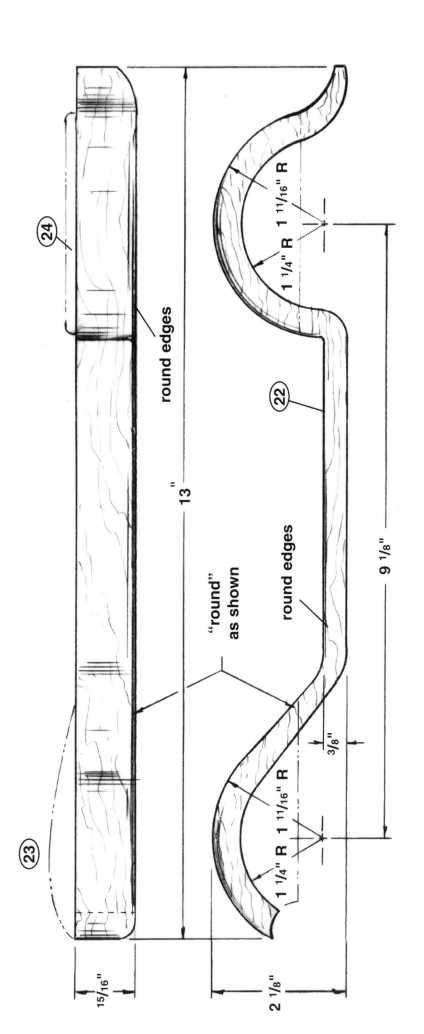

round edges

24

13"

"round" as shown

round edges

1 1/4" R   1 11/16" R

22

3/8"

9 1/8"

23

1 1/4" R   1 11/16" R

15/16"

2 1/8"

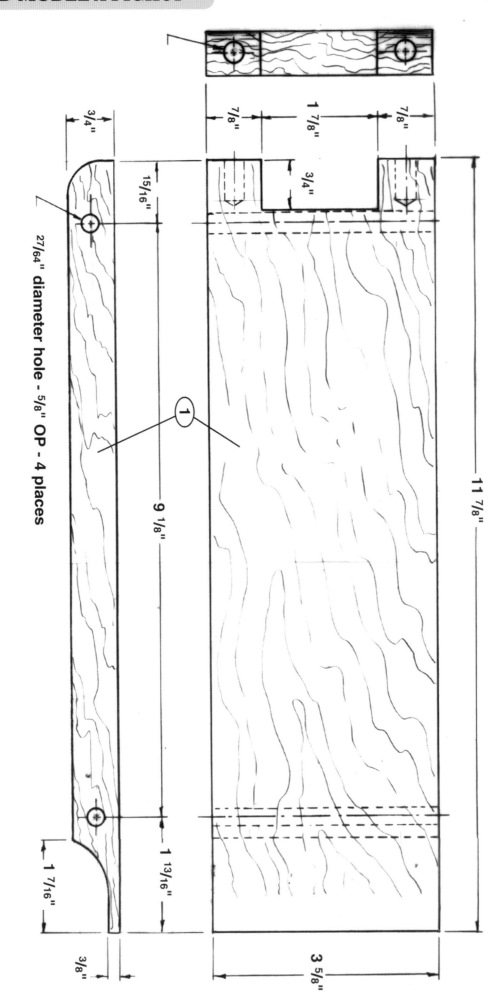

27/64" diameter hole - 5/8" OP - 4 places

3/4"

15/16"

7/8"

1 7/8"

7/8"

3/4"

11 7/8"

9 1/8"

1 13/16"

1 7/16"

3/8"

3 5/8"

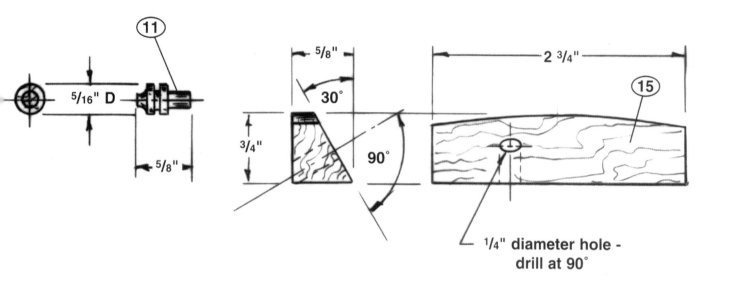

¹/₄" diameter hole -
drill at 90°

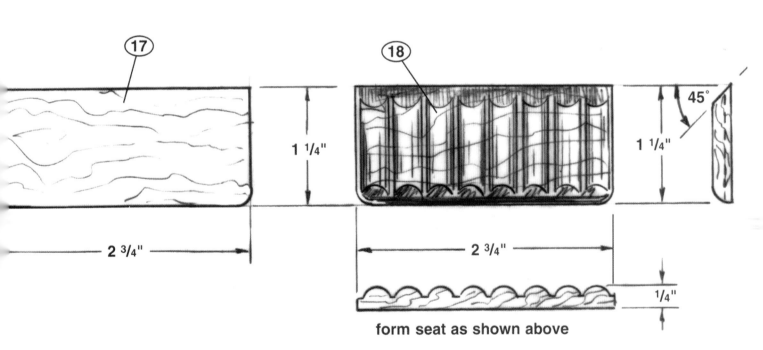

form seat as shown above

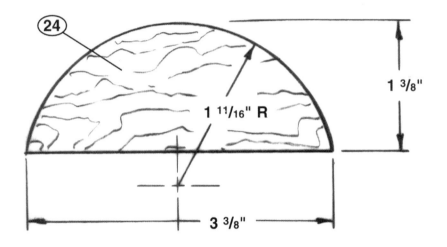

24

1 $^{11}/_{16}$" R

1 $^{3}/_{8}$"

3 $^{3}/_{8}$"

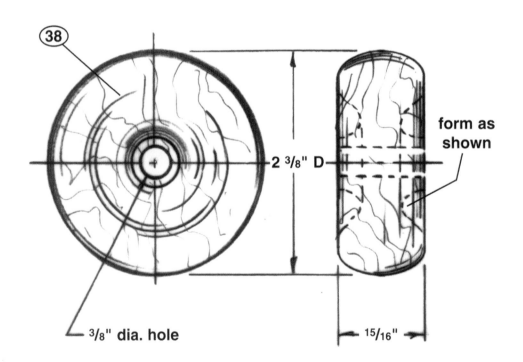

38

2 $^{3}/_{8}$" D

form as
shown

$^{3}/_{8}$" dia. hole

$^{15}/_{16}$"

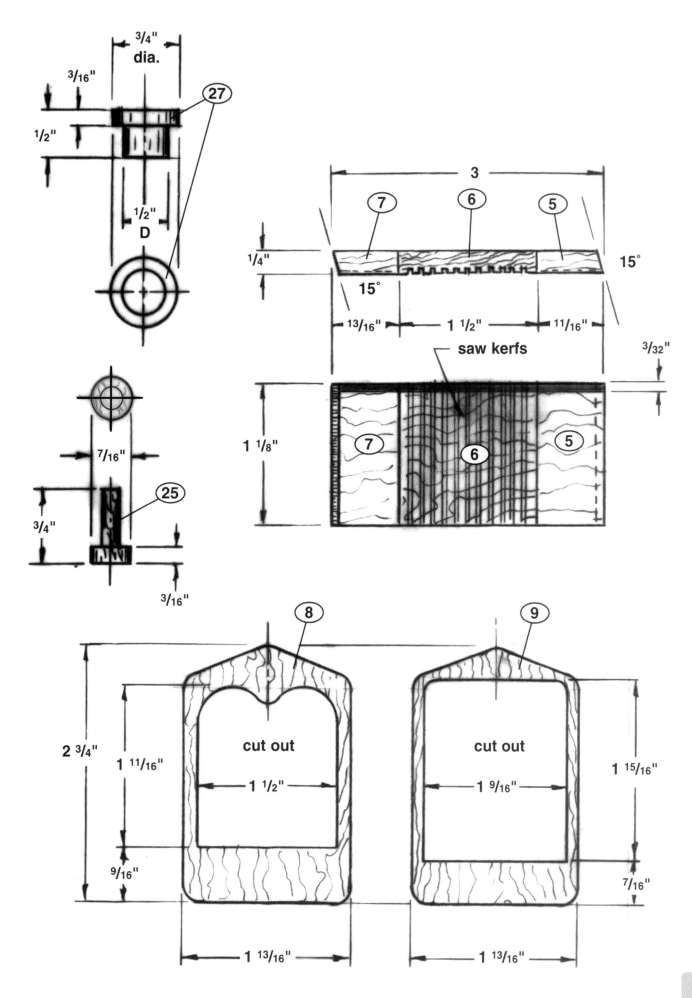

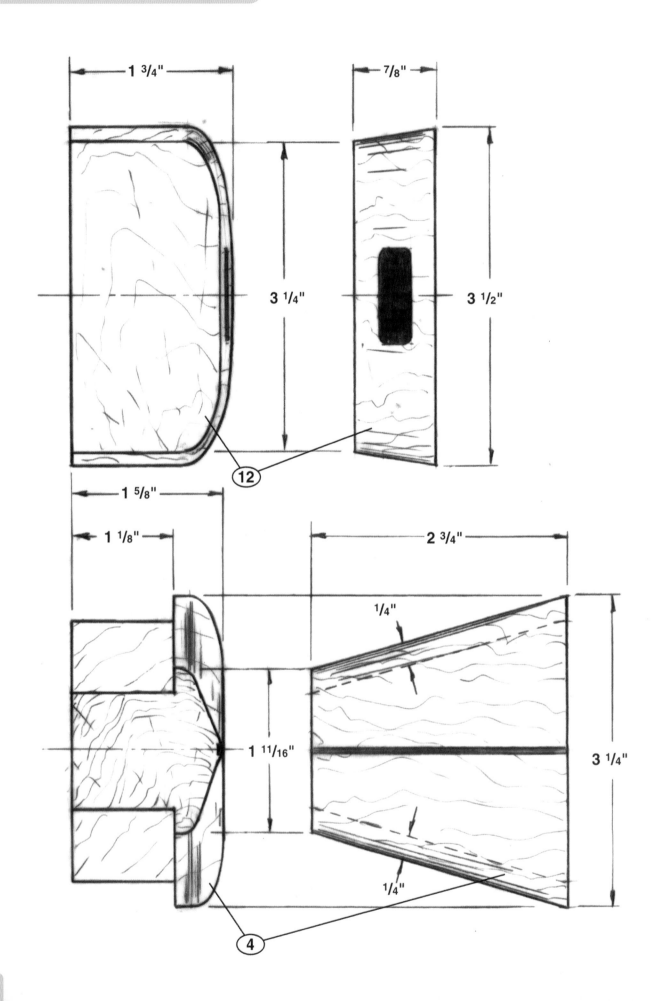

1 3/4"

7/8"

3 1/4"

3 1/2"

12

1 5/8"

1 1/8"

2 3/4"

1/4"

1 11/16"

3 1/4"

1/4"

4

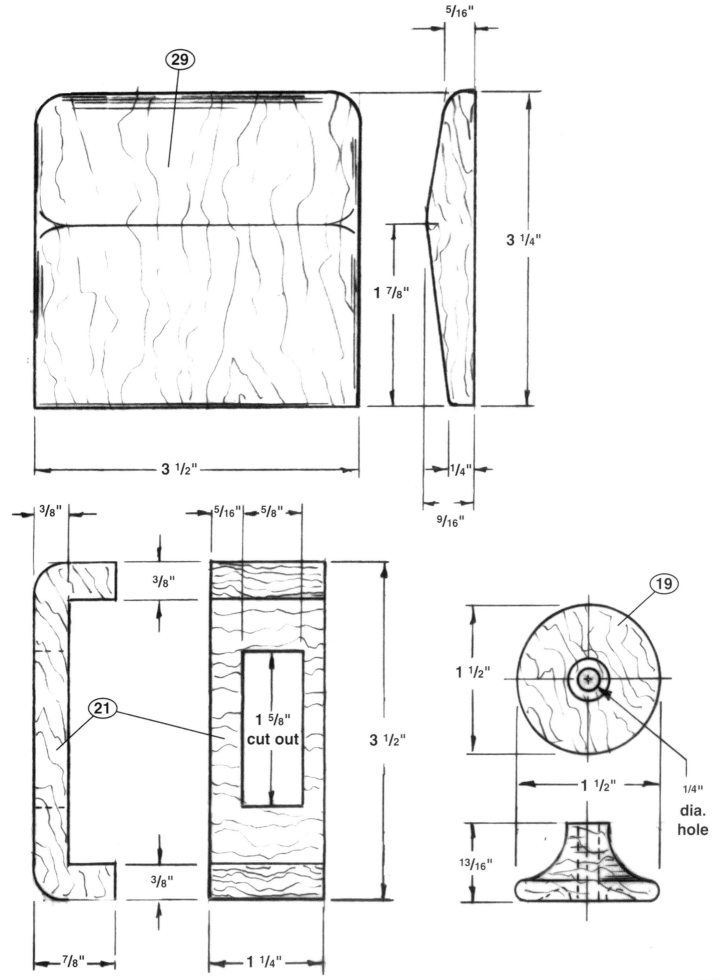

29

5/16"

3 1/4"

1 7/8"

3 1/2"

1/4"

9/16"

3/8"

5/16"   5/8"

3/8"

21

1 5/8"
cut out

3 1/2"

3/8"

7/8"   1 1/4"

19

1 1/2"

1 1/2"

1/4"
dia.
hole

13/16"

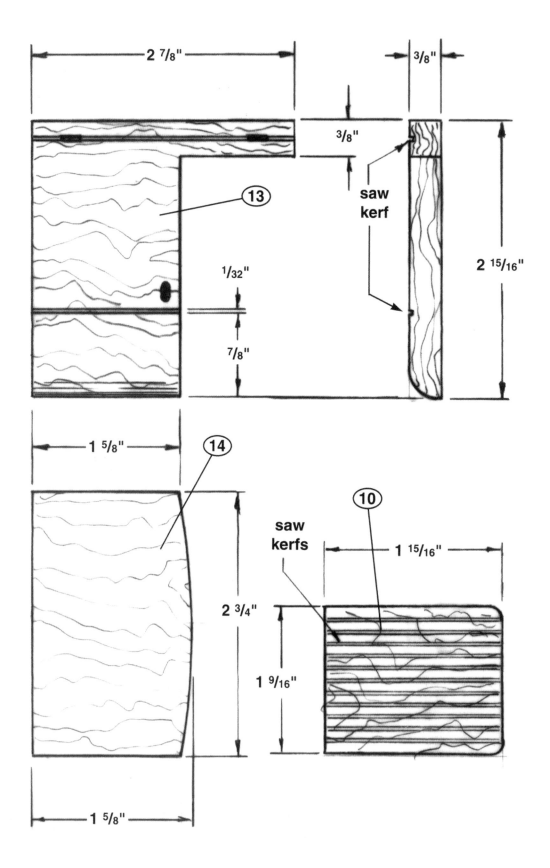

2 7/8"

3/8"

3/8"

saw kerf

13

2 15/16"

1/32"

7/8"

1 5/8"

14

2 3/4"

saw kerfs

10

1 15/16"

1 9/16"

1 5/8"

Flatbed Trailer Parts List

PIECE #	PIECE	SIZE (INCHES)	QUANTITY
1	Base	$7/16 \times 5\frac{3}{4} \times 24$	1
2	Spine	$\frac{1}{4} \times 1\frac{3}{4} \times 23\frac{3}{4}$	1
3	Tool Box	$1\frac{1}{2} \times 1\frac{3}{4} \times 10\frac{1}{4}$	1
4	Axle Housing	$1\,9/16 \times 1\frac{3}{4} \times 2\frac{3}{4}$	2
5	Holder (Large)	$5/16 \times \frac{1}{2} \times 5\frac{3}{4}$	1
6	Mud Guard	$1/32 \times 1\frac{1}{2} \times 1\,15/16$	4
7	Holder (Small)	$5/16 \times \frac{1}{2} \times 1\,15/16$	2
8	Tool Box	$1\frac{1}{2} \times 2\frac{1}{4} \times 5\frac{5}{8}$	1
9	Brace	$\frac{1}{4} \times \frac{1}{4} \times 1\,15/16$	4
10	Support	$\frac{1}{8} \times 5/16 \times 1\frac{1}{2}$	2
11	Brace	$\frac{1}{8} \times 5/16 \times \frac{3}{4}$	2
12	Bumper	$\frac{1}{8} \times \frac{1}{4} \times 2\frac{7}{8}$	1
13a	Outside Lights	$5/16$ Dia. $\times 1/32$	6
13b	Inside Lights	$\frac{1}{4}$ Dia. $\times 1/32$	3
14	Front	$\frac{1}{4} \times 5\frac{3}{4} \times 3$	1
15	Side	$\frac{1}{4} \times 1 \times 2\,9/16$	2
16	Vertical Trim	$1/16 \times 5/16 \times 2\,9/16$	8
17	Front Trim	$1/16 \times 5/16 \times 5\frac{3}{4}$	1
18	Side Trim	$1/16 \times 5/16 \times 1\,1/16$	2
19	Side	$1/16 \times 7/16 \times 24\frac{3}{8}$	2
20	End	$1/16 \times 7/16 \times 5\frac{3}{4}$	2
21	Trailer Hitch	$7/16$ Dia. $\times \frac{7}{8}$	1
22	Brace	$\frac{1}{8}$ Dia. $\times 4\frac{5}{8}$	1
23	Spacer	$\frac{5}{8} \times \frac{3}{4} \times 1\frac{1}{2}$	2
24	Leg	$5/16 \times 5/16 \times 1\frac{5}{8}$	2
25	Bracket	$\frac{1}{8} \times 5/16 \times \frac{3}{4}$	4
26	Foot	$1/16 \times \frac{3}{4} \times \frac{3}{4}$	2
27	Wheel	$2\frac{1}{4}$ Dia. $\times 15/16$	8
28	Axle	$\frac{3}{8}$ Dia. $\times$ Length To Suit	4
29	Hubcap	$\frac{3}{8}$ Dia. Button	8

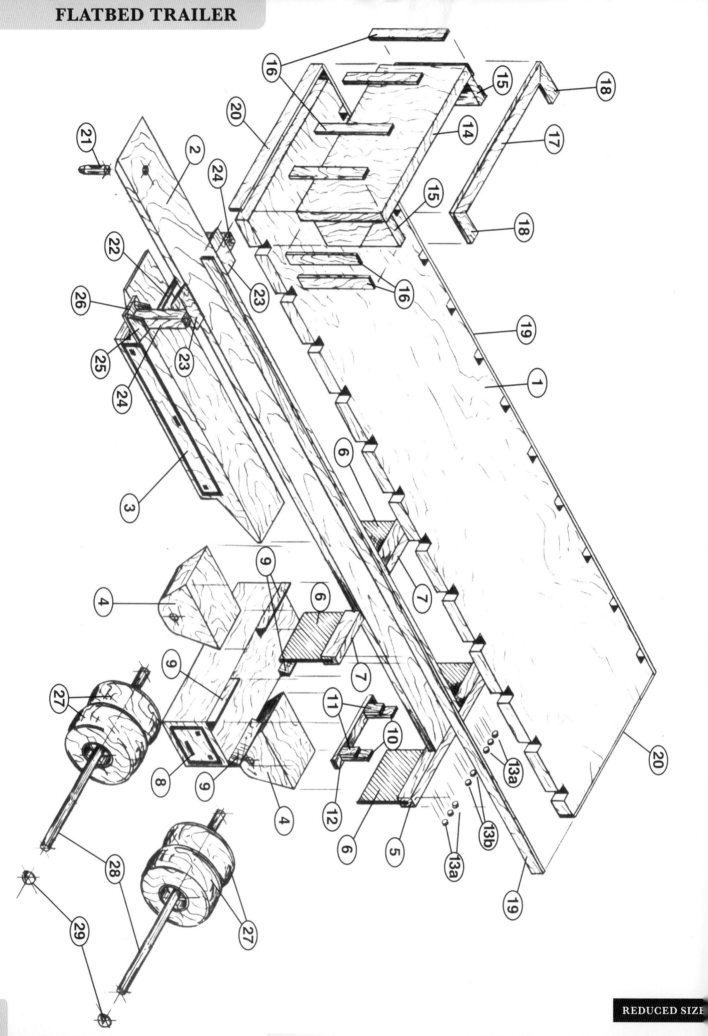

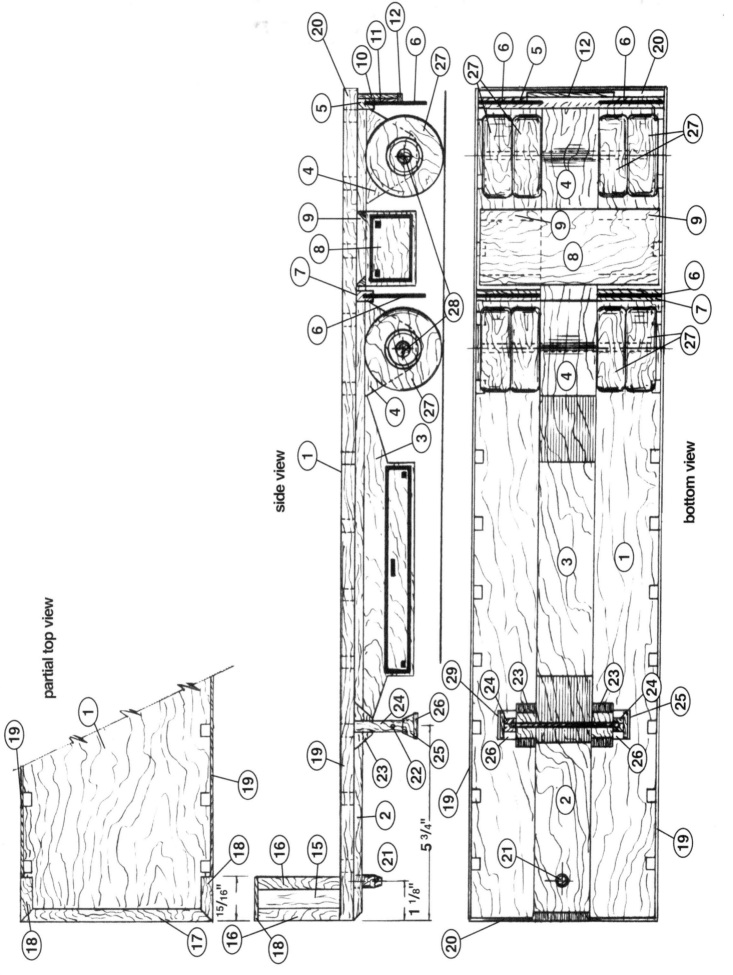

partial top view

side view

bottom view

5 3/4"

1 1/8"

15/16"

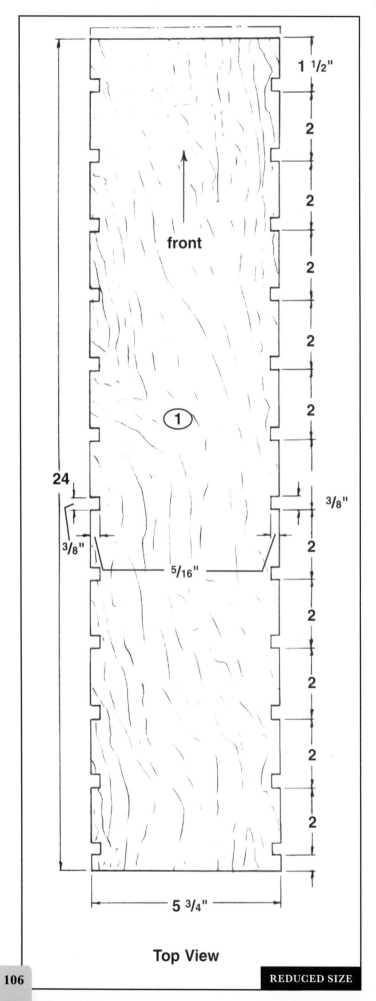

1 1/2"

2

2

2

2

2

2

3/8"

2

5/16"

2

2

2

2

2

24

3/8"

3/8"

front

①

5 3/4"

Top View

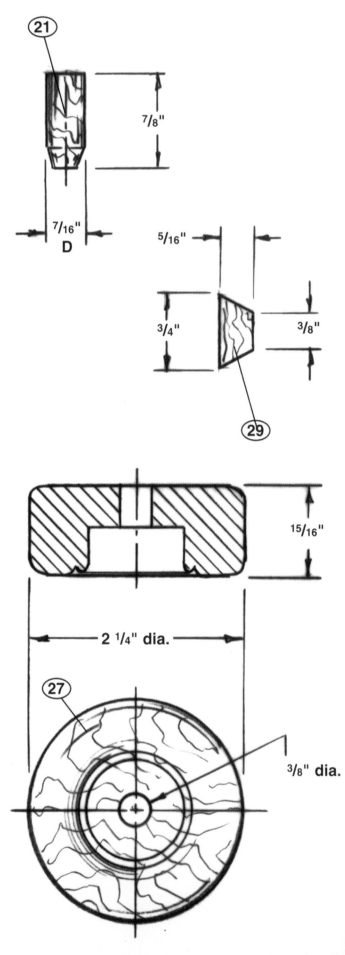

㉑

7/8"

7/16"
D

5/16"

3/4"

3/8"

㉙

15/16"

2 1/4" dia.

㉗

3/8" dia.

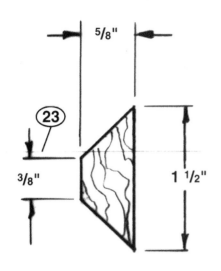

5/8"

23

3/8"

1 1/2"

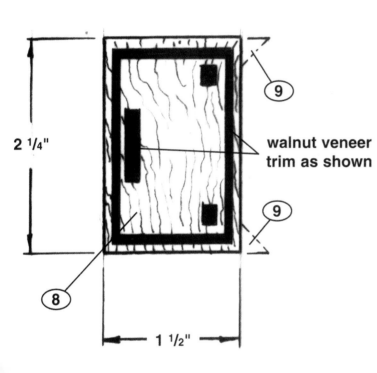

2 1/4"

9

9

8

walnut veneer
trim as shown

1 1/2"

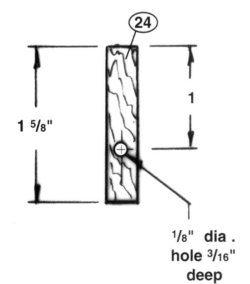

24

1 5/8"

1

1/8" dia .
hole 3/16"
deep

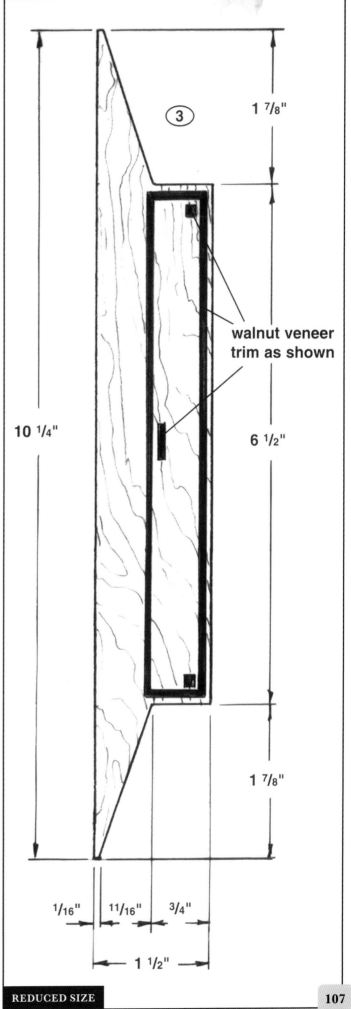

3

1 7/8"

walnut veneer
trim as shown

10 1/4"

6 1/2"

walnut veneer
trim as shown

1 7/8"

1/16"   11/16"   3/4"

1 1/2"

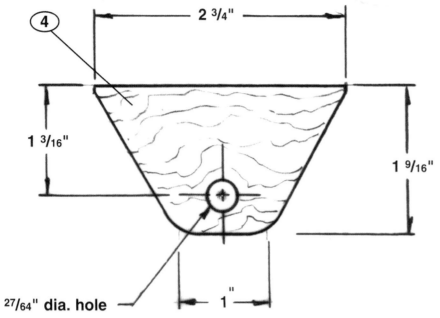

④

2 3/4"

1 3/16"

1 9/16"

27/64" dia. hole

1"

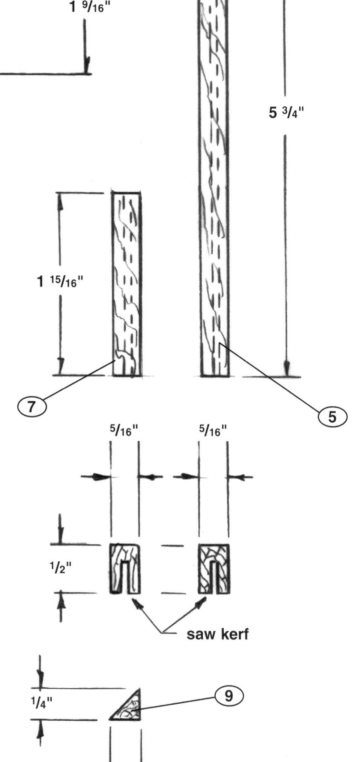

5 3/4"

1 15/16"

⑦

⑤

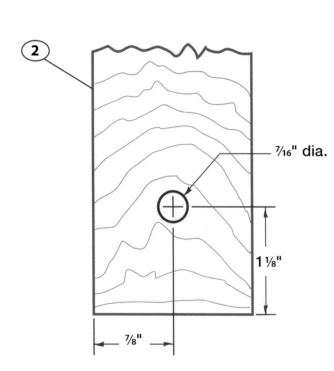

②

7/16" dia.

1 1/8"

7/8"

5/16"

5/16"

1/2"

saw kerf

1/4"

⑨

1/4"

APPENDIX

Information on Making Tambours

"Tambour Cabinet Doors," Richard Wedler, *Fine Woodworking* magazine, March/April 1993, issue no. 99.

Source for Hole Saws and Tambours

Rockler Woodworking and Hardware
1-800-279-4441
www.rockler.com

Best Choices for Stationary Power Tools

Many tools on the market today can be used to create collectable toys. The following list includes the author's suggestions for in-shop power tools.

- Table saw

- Drill press

- Lathe

- Jointer

- Thickness planer

- Belt and disk sander

- Oscillating drum sander

- Router table

- Radial arm saw

Metric Equivalents

EQUATION

To calculate the exact millimeter equivalent for a given figure in inches, simply multiply the inches by 25.4. So, 5" = 127mm; 5¼" = 133.35mm (which can typically be rounded to the nearest whole millimeter).

QUICK REFERENCE EQUIVALENTS

⅛"	3mm
¼"	6mm
⅜"	9mm
½"	12mm
⅝"	16mm
¾"	19mm
⅞"	22mm
1"	25mm

COMMON DIMENSIONAL LUMBER EQUIVALENTS

Sizes: Metric cross sections are so close to their U.S. sizes, as noted below, that for most purposes they may be considered equivalents.

1 x 2	19 x 38mm
1 x 4	19 x 89mm
2 x 2	38 x 38mm
2 x 4	38 x 89mm
2 x 6	38 x 140mm
2 x 8	38 x 184mm
2 x 10	38 x 235mm
2 x 12	38 x 286mm

ABOUT THE AUTHORS

Sam Martin

ven as a farm boy, Sam Martin had an interest in making toys. Although the early ones were crudely made and nailed
gether, Sam never lost the desire to build better toys. It was in the early 1980s that he and his son invested in shop tools.
am built some furniture at first, but he soon devoted his time to making reproductions of trucks, cars, steam shovels,
d backhoes.

During his entire woodworking career, Sam, a retired biochemist, scaled down some fifty different vehicles and excavators.
over a decade and a half, he crafted nearly 3,000 toys.

Roger Schroeder

oger Schroeder's success as a writer began when he failed to write the great American novel. Instead, he turned to writing
out his hobby: woodworking. Sharpening his writing skills and his photography and expanding his interests, he went on to
uthor thirteen books and some eighty magazine articles. Ranging in scope from woodcarving to house building, the books
clude titles such as *How to Carve Wildfowl*, *Making Wood Signs*, and *Timber Frame Construction*.

Despite the prolific output, this was not Roger's full-time profession. Before his retirement, he was a high school English
acher, specializing in teaching writing and research.

When Roger was not teaching, he lectured on topics such as how to make wood into furniture, houses, and sculpture. In the
maining time, he was an amateur cabinetmaker—specializing in Victorian reproductions—and an amateur bird carver who
s received a number of blue ribbons for his natural wood sculptures.

INDEX

Note: Page numbers in **bold** indicate gallery photos/captions. Page numbers in *italics* indicate projects.